Power Up

Power Up

Taking Charge of Your Financial Destiny

Howard S. Dvorkin, CPA

WILEY

Cover image: Debra Todd
Cover design: Paul McCarthy

For general information on our other products and services or for technical support, please contact our Customer Care Department within the United States at (800) 762-2974, outside the United States at (317) 572-3993 or fax (317) 572-4002.

Wiley publishes in a variety of print and electronic formats and by print-on-demand. Some material included with standard print versions of this book may not be included in e-books or in print-on-demand. If this book refers to media such as a CD or DVD that is not included in the version you purchased, you may download this material at http://booksupport.wiley.com. For more information about Wiley products, visit www.wiley.com.

Library of Congress Cataloging-in-Publication Data:

Dvorkin, Howard S.
    Power up : taking charge of your financial destiny / Howard S. Dvorkin.
      pages   cm
    Includes index.
    ISBN 978-1-118-73149-9 (paper); ISBN 978-1-118-78056-5 (cloth);
    ISBN 978-1-118-73141-3 (ebk); ISBN 978-1-118-73152-9 (ebk)
      1. Consumer credit. 2. Finance, Personal. 3. Debt.
  4. Budgets, Personal. I. Title.
HG3755.D874 2013
332.024–dc23

          2013014157

Printed in the United States of America
10 9 8 7 6 5 4 3 2 1

*I dedicate this book to all of the millions of people
I have come across over the last few decades who have allowed
me to impact their lives in a positive way.
To April Lewis-Parks and Brian Bienkowski for all of their
assistance and research to help produce a product that
I can be proud of.
To my family, who are as always my strength,
my passion, my being . . .*

Contents

Contents

Introduction

Now that you have opened this book and are taking the time to read this introduction, I want you to think of this as a new day, a new beginning, a new journey, and a new you. Your past financial difficulties are just that—in the past; they are over with and done. It's time to take control of your financial and personal life and I'm going to help you do that.

We are officially a team working toward the goal of getting you back on your feet, confident in your ability to handle your finances and thrive in this unpredictable world. Stick with me and I'll help you be a better money manager and give you tips on how to ignore the myriad of outside influences that persuade people to spend money.

I realize money is important, but how you spend it and what you spend it on is more important. You will come to learn that and realize, as you continue to read, that you are not alone in this journey. Millions of Americans have suffered some sort of financial turmoil. Some fight back to regain control of their lives and some don't. You are a fighter. You want your life back. We are going to take some punches along the way but we are going to keep swinging, keep fighting, and working toward your goal.

You are your own person. You don't need to impress anyone; you simply need the courage and the guidance to see this journey to the end. I know you have the courage and I will supply you with the guidance. So let's make the commitment to fight together and finish this freedom quest.

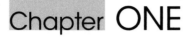

Chapter ONE

The Path That Led You Here

Okay, it's happened. You've lost your financial freedom and now you have to start making changes to get back on your feet. It's easy to make excuses, and there may be some legitimate issues that spurred your run of bad luck. You may have lost your job or were confronted by medical bills that you just couldn't pay. That happens in life and it doesn't seem fair. Unfortunately "fair" plays a minuscule role in the world of personal finances. Regardless of the reason, now, not later, is the first day of your financial life and you need to take charge. You and only you must be in charge from this day forward.

If you're reading this book, debt, spending, and overall unfortunate cash management probably prompted your tumble off the cliff. You're not alone. Millions of people take that same fall every year. In this country debt is as prevalent as shopping malls, but the insidious thing is you don't see it—you don't advertise or brag about it. You keep debt to yourself. You sit in your bed at night thinking about it, wondering how it got this bad. The debt is always there, like a bad habit that's nearly impossible to break. You hide it as best as you can because you don't want anyone to find out. It's somewhat embarrassing, and it's frustrating because most people don't know what to do about it once it occurs. You didn't mean to get into debt; there was no plan—"Hey, I think I'll get into debt this year." Some folks even rationalize debt as part of our culture, by thinking that everybody is in debt.

Most people don't wake up to find themselves anchored by debt. Debt is usually a slow accumulation (unless you recently purchased a new house or incurred an immense expense) caused by purchasing products, services, or other things that you may have not needed or expected. With that being said, let's investigate and discuss the factors that may have helped cause your financial situation.

Who the Heck Are the Joneses, and Why Are You Trying to Keep Up with Them?

Most of us don't like to think of ourselves as materialistic or competitive consumers trying to keep up with our neighbors, friends, and work associates. But face it, when the guy at work drives up in a new Lexus and you're driving a six-year-old car, that pang of envy is real. You start to wonder how on earth he got the money to buy a luxury car—and yes, think about the words we use to describe cars: hot, awesome, cool. Maybe you start to associate those words with the owner. He may not have been cool last week, but with everyone checking out his new wheels he certainly fits the description now.

That feeling is natural, but it doesn't mean you have to buy a new car. Most people won't, but they may start to check out prices for new cars just to get familiar with the market. The car becomes a status symbol, just as does a cup of java from a gourmet coffee shop. Everyone knows where the coffee came from because the logo is prominently displayed on the cup. I understand that comparing the purchase of a cup of coffee and a car is a stretch, but the point is that these things are being observed by you and by others. Maybe you were purchasing coffee at a local coffee shop for a dollar cheaper each morning, but now that you notice everyone at work with their gourmet brands you decide to do the same. You just increased your spending outflow by five dollars each week, or $260 each year. It may not seem significant, but you know things tend to accumulate.

It's somewhat sad that what was deemed a simple household staple has been transformed into a status symbol. I take my hat off to the marketers who branded Starbucks. When a simple cup of coffee defines who you are and where you are going in life, it becomes apparent that we are in trouble as a society. Think about it for a second—does a cup of coffee from McDonald's exude a feeling of luxury like a cup of coffee from Starbucks? The coffee beans are probably comparable and may have come from the same farm in Colombia or wherever they were grown, but the logo on the cup makes all the difference—it signifies status. Yep, we are in trouble.

That's how easily the "keeping up with the Joneses" dilemma begins. If you're a woman you probably know what kind of perfume, lipstick, clothes, and shoes your friends wear. If they are buying brand labels then you probably are too, even if you don't make the same amount of money as they do. A woman I work with confided that she would never think of showing up to a party in anything other than a suitable brand label. That got me thinking, she used the word "suitable," which means among other things: adapted to a use or purpose, qualified, proper. She needed to feel equipped to be among that company. If she did not wear the designer clothing, then she may become unqualified or unfit to be in such company. The pressure in her mind to wear that clothing was enormous, enough to make her spend beyond her means and, as she told me later during a cathartic moment, enough to make her go into serious debt. You see, it's that simple. If you happen to associate with people who make more money and you want to keep up with them, then you may become desperate and start using your credit cards for things that you simply cannot afford. It's a trap. Nobody purposely laid the trap, but our society has evolved into this dilemma, and we are the victims. As a result, we are going broke trying to maintain our memberships in a perceived class of people.

Men are no different. The large majority of them may not be fascinated with clothes and jewelry, but just talk to them about their "toys." They will be happy to entertain you by chattering about their top-of-the-line golf clubs, fishing equipment, electronics, cars, motorcycles, even garden equipment. If a neighbor down the road purchases a John Deere riding mower, you can be sure most of the men have seen it or heard about it. Again, it doesn't mean all the men in the neighborhood will rush out to buy a riding mower, but they may take a peek at the push mower in their garage and start wondering what it would take to replace it.

Adding to the Cart

Most of us have seen it: you order something online and the next thing you know the manufacturer or web site such as Amazon is immediately luring you into another purchase—adding to the cart. I've seen it where you are one click away from checking out and the retailer throws one or two last offers at you. Intrusive—yes. Obnoxious—yes. Smart—absolutely. From the retailers' standpoint, they are trying to get one last bite of the apple. That doesn't only happen online, though. It happens when you purchase a set of earrings and suddenly notice the pendent that goes with those earrings or the wallet that fits perfectly with your new handbag. It never ends. If you buy an MP3 player or a cellphone you can get a waterproof case, in the event that you absolutely need to speak with someone while lounging in the tub or pool!

Adding to the cart is one way to get into serious debt. Just think about it: Almost everything that you buy has an accessory. If you own a guitar, then you have to have a case, guitar picks, a strap, song books, and extra strings; if it's electric, then you need an amp, cords, and maybe a fancy gizmo that changes the sound of the guitar while you're playing it. It's nearly impossible to buy one thing without getting a half dozen other things that add to the price.

The other day I was in a national sporting goods store buying boots, bindings, and a snowboard for my kids. It took some time, but with help from a fellow shopper and the salesperson, I found what I thought was the perfect equipment. Upon finalizing the sale, the clerk tells me I should get "insurance" for the snowboard. Amazingly, the cost of the insurance matched to the penny the savings I received from the discounted sale price. Of course I said no thanks and inquired why I would need insurance on a snowboard. The answer I received was interesting. The sales clerk told me the insurance covers the board if it cracks. The fact is that the board is designed not to crack. It is meant to take a beating. The sales clerk justified trying to sell me insurance saying it includes one free waxing of the board, which costs the same as the insurance.

Here's the funny part. The free waxing had to be done immediately upon purchase. The board already came with a factory coat of wax, which is probably better than what the store would put on it. More importantly, if I wanted the upgraded coating rather than the plain old wax, that was more money. You see what I mean—so much for being free.

Say you are about to shell out $2,000 for a 60-inch flat-screen TV that can be mounted on the wall. You're probably psyching yourself up thinking, that's not too bad; I can probably afford those monthly payments. Then you realize the wall mounts cost extra, and the latest and greatest cables (to give you the clearest picture possible) are also extra. Then there is the surround-sound system that will fill your room with exquisite sounds. Why not go for that, right? I mean if you are going to do it, do it right the first time. (People actually say these things to themselves. Maybe you remember saying it.) When you get the total charge, that original $2,000 has been blown out of the water. Between the TV, cables, wall-mount brackets, surround-sound system, and the dreaded sales tax, you're at $3,000. Now, who has the guts to walk away? The salesperson entices you further by offering an interest-free credit card to put the purchase on. Wow! That's awesome. Not really. What the salesperson neglected to tell you or maybe didn't realize, and you didn't read the terms of the offer, is that after 12 months if you don't pay the balance off in full the interest is tacked on at a rate of 28%. That's from day one of the purchase date and going forward! Great deal? Probably not—after you get done making the minimum payments over the next eight years and have paid for the merchandise about two and a half times over. That's it right there in a nutshell for many people. They can't say no. They are in the present, they are excited, and they have already talked themselves into making the purchase. All the salesperson has to do is give a reassuring smile and join the excitement. Heck, they'll even congratulate you. Remember, that's their job, to sell the product and to sell the joy of the purchase. You won't hear a salesperson ask if you'll be able to afford these products six months down the road. That's up to you to figure out *before* you enter the store or go online.

Emotional Buying

I have a story for you. A friend of mine went through a divorce a while back. The split up was not contentious, but it did leave him wracked with guilt. You see, his son was just turning 13 and my friend thought he should be there for him and do a father-and-son thing together, to help him through this difficult and confusing time. Because of work he could rarely see him during the week but he did have time on the weekends. My friend thought that it would be a great idea to buy his son a dirt bike. He was handy with engines and he conjured up images of him and his son sharing great times together, getting dirty and greasy, and really having a ball. There was a place not too far from the apartment he was renting where they could take the bike out.

He had $1,500 saved and put that toward a $4,000 dirt bike—yes, $4,000. He apparently did not do his homework and found that the dirt bikes his son favored were delivered in what the motorcycle world calls "race ready"—meaning the manufacturer used state-of-the-art components, from the shocks to the handlebars. What my friend also didn't count on were the accessories added to the "cart": a helmet, motorcycle boots, gloves, eye protection, and a jersey with the company's logo and colors. After all was said and done, he took a loan out for around $3,000. It was a loan he couldn't afford, but in his mind he just couldn't let his son down.

Now let me make it clear that his son did not ask for the bike; he did not make his father feel guilty or less of a father because they couldn't share those motorcycle moments together. As a matter of fact the dirt bike was a surprise gift. My friend was so caught up in his emotions, the feelings of guilt and worthlessness as a father and husband, that he lost sight of reality—financial and personal. He never sat down and fully thought out the money that he would be spending and the consequences. It's a sad story really. He couldn't afford to keep the bike and it was repossessed, which left him spiraling further into depression from the embarrassment of his financial challenges being communicated to his child courtesy of the repo man.

A number of things can set people off on a spending binge, from guilt to sheer irresponsibility, from sadness to a sense of entitlement. You know how it goes; you had a tough week at work so on the weekend you splurge on clothes, jewelry, sporting equipment, the latest electronic gadget, or whatever turns you on. You deserve it, right? (Maybe you deserve it, but that's not the point, is it? The real point is, can you afford it? That's what you should be asking yourself.) There is actually a name for this type of thinking: It's called "retail therapy." You rationalize why you deserve that new coat or pair of shoes when you already have coats and shoes. What you should do— and listen very carefully—is take a deep breath and calm yourself down. Think clearly and ask yourself whether you really need those things. The bottom line is that you don't and you're only damaging your finances and yourself because you are spending while your emotions are running at a fever pitch. The best suggestion is to stay out of the stores all together unless you have a specific item to purchase. If that is the case, find what you need and get out the front door as fast as you can. Walking around a store aimlessly is going to cost you money because the chance of your buying something you don't need is extremely high. Run, don't walk.

Everyone gets emotional, and it doesn't matter if the emotion is sadness or happiness—you want to respond to it. If you are sad, you want to find a cure for it and for many shopping is a temporary fix. But after the shopping and spending is done, you look at what you bought and the money spent and you find that you're still not happy. You may have been temporarily pleased with yourself while shopping, but the aftermath is a disaster. If you are happy you want to share that happiness, maybe celebrate by buying something you don't need and can't afford. Once you realize what you have done, that happiness quickly evaporates. You see, emotional buying is a losing business; you can't win. It's important to stop and think clearly before you react to the emotion. If you are sad, perhaps you can call a friend, play a game, or go for a walk with your pet. Do something that doesn't cost you.

Buying What You Can't Maintain

This is the money needed for expenses you incur, but you don't think about or realize it until it's too late. Let me explain: I was driving down the road the other day and watched a young man pass me in a huge truck he had tricked out. You've seen those trucks—lifted five feet off the ground, behemoth tires, and two pairs of shocks for each wheel, with fancy rims and an exhaust system that creates a deafening roar. What stood out though were the tires; they were nearly bald, and I mean so worn down that belts of metal were visible. I came to a conclusion—he couldn't afford new tires. What started out as a great idea, at least to him, purchasing tires that probably cost $300 to $400 apiece, now became a financial burden that posed a safety risk. I began to notice other trucks and SUVs with tires worn down to unsafe levels. There's no reason not to replace your tires, especially when you are carting your loved ones around. Laziness, maybe? Trying to save a buck? I don't buy it. Too many people purchase things without thinking about how much it is going to cost to maintain them properly.

Maybe you've done the same thing and it cost you in ways other than financial. It not only costs you money but it also costs you sleep and even a sense of decency. A person in my insurance agent's office lived in a house he couldn't maintain because he could barely afford the mortgage. His landscaping became a mess, the paint on the house started to fade and chip, and the pool morphed into a mosquito retreat. Neighbors started to complain and he and his family felt embarrassed. It was all because (by his own admission) he wanted to live in a certain neighborhood and live up to certain standards. He could get the mortgage but he never thought further ahead, or maybe he didn't want to think further ahead, about how he would maintain such a house and its trappings. Well, those trappings caught him and it cost him dearly. These are the financial burdens that you bear if you don't use your head and seriously realize that there is always a price to pay. You have to find the price that suits your monetary situation.

Think about the things that people buy and maybe you bought that must be maintained. The list could nearly be infinite, but we'll take on a dozen or so: pets, pools, hot tubs, motorcycles, cars, landscaping, motorhomes, firearms, computers, boats, vacation homes, lawn mowers, appliances, sporting equipment, clothing. Let's not forget, although you do not buy them of course, children. When you have a child you immediately have to spend more money to take care of her or him. So you get the picture. Think before you buy. Remember that once the purchase is made you will probably have to sink more money into that product to keep it functioning properly. Once you pay the price of acquisition you have to pay again and again. It never ends.

We will elaborate on these subjects later in the book. For now, I want you to start thinking positive and consider how you can become a better money manager. First, though, I want to introduce you to a major influence that persuades you to spend.

The Influence of Advertising

From the moment we wake to the moment we rest our heads on a pillow, we are barraged by advertising. Every waking moment we are confronted with some type of communication telling us how we are supposed to look. What to spend our money on. What we need to buy and why. Yes, advertising is influencing this culture, and unfortunately negatively influencing our finances and ultimately our outlook. It is changing the way we think and what we will have in the future in regards to resources.

For example: How can anyone in America possibly leave their house or function throughout the day without a bottled water? Bottled water is safer, it keeps our hunger satiated so we won't want to eat more food, and as a consequence it makes us healthier. That's the message and I'm sure you've heard it or read it. Oh, and don't forget that many health professionals recommend that we drink at least eight glasses of water a day to ensure healthy skin and body hydration. The truth is that there is no concrete science that backs that claim. Sure, it's okay to drink water, but if you want a cheeseburger all the water in the world is not going to prevent you from eating that burger. Just think about all those plastic bottles that aren't recycled; they sit in landfills for an eternity or litter our streets and waterways. What happened to tap water? Think about it—you are *buying* water. You may even be buying tap water in a plastic bottle. Seriously, one of the largest brands of bottled water clearly states on the label in small print that the product is derived from the New York City Public Works Department.

Advertisers are professional persuaders. They are paid to stimulate your "buying mechanism." We all have this mechanism; it goes off in our brain and in our heart and it tells us that we need that product, whether it's bottled water or an SUV. Look at how many Americans bought into the SUV message—it's safer for you and your family (especially your kids) and you can fit the whole neighborhood in the back seats along with the groceries; how convenient. Every family should have one, and heck you can see over everyone else because the seats are so high up. After you drive an SUV you'll never be able to go back to a little car—you won't feel secure. What the advertisers didn't tell you was that these vehicles get terrible gas mileage and their cost is sometimes exorbitant, although you can lease one for a sweet deal, as long as you qualify and don't dare go over the mileage limit. Of course, the dealer will penalize you if you try to get out of the lease. It's there, I assure you. Don't be fooled. Nothing in this world is free. If you notice, some of the worst drivers on the road are SUV people. They barrel down the road as if they were driving a sports car. That's because they think they really are safe and that nothing can hurt them. They bought into the image created by the advertisers, even if they couldn't afford the vehicle. You see, the advertisers persuaded them that they could not afford to *not* buy the vehicle. Parents with one or two kids lumber down the road in these monsters even if they are over their heads in debt. How do they afford the gas? Put it on the credit card. How do they afford to pay for those huge tires when they are worn down? Put it on the credit card. Now, I'm not trying to make generalizations here. Some people can afford expensive SUVs, but I think there is enough evidence and enough people trading in their SUVs because they couldn't afford the gas or maintenance to make the statement.

Think about advertising or selling methods at your grocery store. As I approach my grocery store I can smell fresh-baked goods. In Paco Underhill's book *Why We Buy: The Science of Shopping*, he calls the first few steps into a retail store the "transition zone." It's where shoppers transition from the outside world to the retail space. In my grocery store the bakery is to the left, and it has fresh-baked bread for sale in bins about 15 feet in front of me as I walk into the store. Like most other shoppers, I grab a loaf even if I don't need it, because I rapidly think to myself of the multiple ways I can use that loaf—for dinner, sandwiches, breakfast. I am then funneled off to the left, where the bakery and other products are located. Only the most determined and focused shoppers will take a detour to the right or go straight past the bins and find the exact aisle where the exact product they need is located. Those shoppers probably have a list and are intent not to pick up extra items that they don't need. Lesson learned: Make a list and stick to it; you'll save money and time.

Advertisers tell us that the cereals they are peddling are great for your kids, and they have commercials of kids laughing at the breakfast table to prove it. The sun is shining and mom is happy not harried trying to get to work or get the kids to school. Everything is wonderful and the kids are getting a nutritious meal, right? Maybe that happens on television, but in my house it's pure havoc with yelling, screaming, rushing, and the occasional threat of harsh discipline from medieval times! What about all that sugar and corn syrup and the lack of protein and fiber? Advertisers don't want you to think too hard—don't read the ingredients; just think of the convenience and the happy expression your child will have while filling up on sugar. You don't want advertisers telling you what to buy. You need to manage your money and educate yourself on products, and you need to come to grips with how you spend your money.

It doesn't end with commercials. Think about the television shows you and your kids watch. Kids watch shows where young girls, probably between 10 and 13, dress in the very latest fashions. Now they want the same clothes and they don't want us to buy from Kmart. No, that designates a cheaper style of clothing, not name brands. Many parents fall prey to their kid's insistent pressure and buy fashions they can't afford. Maybe they'll get a store credit card and charge it. The kids are happy but the parents are left struggling to pay the bill. Television shows may influence you in the same manner. If you're a man and you watch golf and see the top golfers with name-brand shirts and clubs, you probably want the same thing. I've seen NASCAR fans (men and women) modify their cars or trucks to look like their favorite driver's car. That can cost a small fortune. It happens; television coerces us to buy certain products and certain "looks"—as in fashion design. What about product placement of items in movies or on television shows? Advertising is everywhere and you don't even know it. It is subliminal and your subconscious is absorbing the message of "buy me" loud and clear.

Advertisers build brand identity, like Nike and the swoosh. It's called brand recognition, and advertisers want you to be loyal to that brand. NASCAR is a brand; so is the NFL, just like Gucci or Chanel. They want you to covet their brand, and that is very dangerous for a consumer at all levels. It's what we've been talking about all along—this desire to have something, to need this product regardless of the cost. You know you really can't afford it, but that doesn't matter. Other people have it and are enjoying it, so why can't you? That's an out-of-control buyer's mentality. A girlfriend has just purchased a Coach bag and is showing it off. If you are a woman and also love Coach bags, then your heart rate is going wild and you can't wait to go buy one. After all, these bags say something about a person. The brand describes you and it gives you a sense of worth, which makes you feel good. Of course, when you get the credit card bill and only have enough money to make a minimum payment or no payment at all, then that sense of worth goes out the window.

You don't have to be loyal to any brand. Try buying grocery store–brand products. Most of them are no different from the name brands and are less expensive. They may even be produced in the same factories as the name brand but with different packaging. They also don't pay excessive costs for packaging—notice how plain their packaging is. And if you are worried about what your neighbors or friends might say if they see those products in your pantry, I have two words for you—who cares! That's right, who cares. You are out to build your own brand—a brand-new you who is smarter and savvier and understands that money is worth more than its monetary value. You are out to build yourself back up from financial crises.

Let's use the cliché that money doesn't grow on trees. We've all heard that a million times, but it is the truth. Money is a precious commodity, and I want you to start thinking that way. Money is not earned just to buy and accumulate material things, as advertisers would like you to believe, and it may or may not buy peace of mind. Money is to be earned, respected, and saved so that when an emergency does occur, or when you need to purchase something that you really do need, you have it.

Okay, so we went over the many reasons why your financial situation went up in flames. Materialism and coveting name-brand products is rampant in America. It's not healthy, financially or otherwise. We know that the purchase, the act of buying is a temporary fix—you feel good while you're doing it but then the bright feelings turn grim after you realize you didn't practice good judgment. Keeping up with the Joneses and adding to the cart is tempting, but it doesn't pay off in the end; it only costs you. Stop for just a moment. Do you really want a materialistic item, whether it's a car or a piece of clothing, to describe you? Aren't you more than that? If you were stripped of all your materialistic possessions, would you be nothing? No, my friend, you are more than the possessions you buy or covet. So now let's move on and learn how you can change your financial habits and your motivations to buy. It's time for the next part of your empowerment.

Chapter TWO

Start to Become Empowered

I don't want to brag, but the reality is I'm a pretty good negotiator. I like it. I have fun with it and I've become very experienced. Negotiating is a big part of what I do for a living. I've also incorporated those same skills into my non-business life. One of the keys is I never take it personally and certainly never get emotionally involved or attached to the negotiation and deal. Frankly speaking, whatever I buy or sell, I really don't care if the deal happens or not. My life is not going to change if I buy, say, a chair or not. The only major benefit I could see under those circumstances is that my beautiful bride will stop telling me how much she hates the existing décor—which may or may not be a contributing factor to my decision. It's certainly not a driving force making me part with the money in my pocket.

There you have it. Don't become attached to the transaction, emotionally or otherwise. Once you are emotionally engaged, you are at a terrible disadvantage. More importantly you need to figure out early on who the boss is—is it the vendor, who is trying to sell you something you probably don't need, or is it you, the guy or gal who the vendor is trying to persuade into spending money? I say it's you, and you need to believe that with the proper conviction. You need to embrace this line of thinking, and no matter how big or small the transaction you must apply this concept in full force and with the necessary belief in yourself. When two parties begin a dialogue about exchanging something and one is totally disengaged and the other is entirely engaged and focused on acquiring what the other party has in their possession, the real strength belongs to the party who is disengaged and holding the currency that the other party desires.

Now you have a better idea of what you're up against. You have credit card companies, advertising professionals, merchandisers, industrial psychologists, your emotions, and your own tendency to spend too much money—and I didn't even mention the occasional bad luck that strikes, like when your car's transmission blows and you need to replace it. It's not easy to save money when it seems like everyone is out to negotiate a way to make you spend it. But it's possible to change and the first couple of things that you need to learn are how to craft a budget and how to become frugal. Remember, you're starting all over; it's a clean slate so do it right the first time. I know there are more entertaining things to do than figuring out how much you make and how much you spend each month. Crafting a budget isn't easy. It's hard. It forces you to be completely honest with yourself and your spending habits and the status of your overall finances.

Crafting a Budget

Crafting a budget is a big deal, so pay careful attention to the data you input and the results generated. It sounds preposterous, but most people don't really know how much money they bring in and how much they spend each month. Even scarier is most don't know exactly how much money they owe. How can they? Most of us are not math whizzes. When you try to add up a house loan, a couple of car loans, six credit cards, and a few floating medical bills it gets tough. That is one of the main reasons why so many people fall into financial turmoil. Once you start spending more than you are making, it's only a matter of time before your finances capsize. Sounds dramatic, right? Well, it is and that's why you're spending time with me reading this book. I want to prepare you and provide you with everything you'll need to be successful.

I'm sure you have heard the saying "The devil is in the details"—meaning that is where the difficulties hide. So don't be nonchalant about building your budget. Be detailed and try to drill down to every last cent. I will provide you with some budget examples, but I want you to customize them to fit your specific financial profile. Don't get lazy on me. This is the beginning, the nuts and bolts and the tools that will build your future. Get excited about it and invite the whole family to take part in crafting the budget. If you're married or live with a significant other and both of you are generating income, then include everything you make together.

Examples of Budget Sheets

Include everything that you make—all sources of *monthly income*. On the following pages is a starter worksheet. Use it and expand it when necessary to include everything. I can't emphasize that point enough—think of all facets of income that you earn. If your children are earning and helping the family out, then add their income to the list. If you are receiving funds from family members or friends, include that as well, regardless of who or where it comes from.

Worksheets for Expenses

Worksheets for expenses come in three categories. Remember, we are being extremely detailed. This will help you understand where all your money is going, thus giving you total control over your spending or nonspending. The three categories are "fixed," "flexible," and "discretionary."

Credit card debt is regarded as a fixed expense even though the payments may fluctuate. If you don't own a credit card currently due to past financial tribulations, include the category in case you decide to apply for one in the future. But don't forget how quickly debt multiplies on a credit card.

Fixed Expenses

Your main fixed expenses are the usual suspects: car payments, mortgage, rent, and so on. These entries usually stay consistent from month to month. Also, notice the entry for credit card debt. If you do own a credit card, take the total monthly credit card payment from the other sheet and enter it.

Monthly Income Worksheet

Monthly Income	Current	Revised
Gross Monthly Income	_____	_____
Gross Monthly Income	_____	_____
Rental Income	_____	_____
Self-Employment Business Income	_____	_____
Interest & Dividend Income	_____	_____
Child Support & Alimony	_____	_____
Other Income	_____	_____
Total Gross Income		

Monthly Taxes	Current	Revised
Federal Taxes	_____	_____
State Taxes	_____	_____
Social Security	_____	_____
Medicare	_____	_____
Total Taxes		

**Net Income =
Total Gross Income –
Total Taxes**

**Cash Flow = Net Income
– Total Expenses**

Revolving Credit Worksheet

Creditor Name	Interest Rate	Balance Owed	Monthly Payment
	%	$	$
	%	$	$
	%	$	$
	%	$	$
	%	$	$
	%	$	$
	%	$	$
	%	$	$
Totals	Average Interest of All Cards: _____ %*	Total Owed: $_____	Total Monthly Credit Card Payment: $_____

*The average interest rate that you attempt to calculate is a very complicated calculation. The end number is a proration of the amount of debt you have and the interest rates that are being applied. For example, you have four cards. The balance of one card is $10,000 and it charges 25 percent interest. The second card has a balance of $5,000 with an interest rate of 20 percent. Card number three is at $2,000 with a 15 percent interest rate, and card number four is $3,000 with a 10 percent rate. Each interest rate applies to a fraction of the total debt, which is $20,000. For example:

10% applies to 3,000/20,000, or 3/20, of the debt.
15% applies to 2,000/20,000, or 1/10, of the debt.
20% applies to 5,000/20,000, or 1/4, of the debt.
25% applies to 10,000/20,000, or 1/5 of the debt.

The calculation would be as follows:

The "weighted" average is given by

$(10\%) \times 3 \div 20 + (15\%) \times 1 \div 10 + (20\%) \times 1 \div 4 + (25\%) \times 1 \div 2$

$= 1.5\% + 1.5\% + 5\% + 12.5\%$

$= 20.5\%$

Note: In this example, the largest amounts of money have the highest interest rates, so the weighted average is high. If the largest amounts of money had the lowest interest rates, the weighted average would be lower.

Fixed Monthly Expenses Worksheet

Monthly Expenses	Current Monthly Fixed Payment
Mortgage/Rent	$
Real Estate Taxes	$
Homeowners Insurance	$
Car Loans/Lease Payments	$
Car Insurance	$
Student Loans	$
Alimony/Child Support	$
Medical Insurance	$
Total Monthly Credit Card Payment (from the credit card worksheet)	$
Other	$
Other	$
Other	$
Total Monthly Fixed Payment	$

Flexible Expenses

Flexible is a perfect way to describe these expenses because most of these expenses will fluctuate monthly.

If you start taking control over your spending, these expenditures will go down significantly almost overnight. You obviously can impact the amount you spend by purchasing groceries that are less expensive, on sale, or are advertised as two-for-one. Similarly, you can save by turning off the lights when you are not in the room or shutting off the TV when you are not watching it; the same goes for your computer: shut it down when you are finished using it. All this can add to your savings.

These small steps accumulate into big savings. There is always an opportunity to spend less money. All you have to do is become inquisitive and proactive. Get more interested in where your money is going and then make a plan to reduce your expenses. Remember, if some of these rows don't apply to you, delete them. If there are other things you are spending money on, say a bimonthly visit to the vet, then divide that amount and add it to the worksheet. The most important thing is that you include everything. Leave nothing out. Overestimate if you have to. Never underestimate, as that leads to problems down the road. Be honest with yourself. If you spend money on something you don't want others to know about, disguise it. Don't ignore it—everything must be included.

In the Flexible Expense worksheet, input the amount you are spending on each expense in the column titled

Flexible Expenses Worksheet

Monthly Expenses	Current Monthly Payment	Amount Allocated for Expense
Telephone Bill	$	$
Electric/Gas/Oil/Fuel Bill	$	$
Cable Television Bill	$	$
Groceries	$	$
Household Supplies	$	$
School Supplies	$	$
Clothes	$	$
Dry Cleaning/Laundry	$	$
Savings *(5% is your starting goal)*		
Other	$	$
Other	$	$
Other	$	$
Total Monthly Flexible Expense	$	$

Current Monthly Payment. The last column is where you are to input the amount you would like to spend on the given expense. For example, if your telephone bill is currently $240 per month and you plan to cut back your plan by $50 per month by reevaluating your options, then you would put $190 in the Amount Allocated for Expense column.

Discretionary Expenses

Okay, we are moving along nicely, but let's see how you do on this next set of expenses. Now I want you to list your discretionary expenses. These are the items that all of us don't necessarily need to comfortably exist but we purchase them anyway. This may become tricky because these expenses fall through the cracks sometimes or get ignored. They may be small items, but even small expenditures add up over time. The most common reason why people overlook these expenditures is that people don't like to confess to spending money on such items; it makes them feel foolish and uncomfortable and sometimes they are being secretive. What I mean is a spouse may not want to admit that he or she spent $50 on something that wasn't necessary, so he or she conveniently forgets about the purchase. This may not pertain to you or your family, but it's a lesson in using discipline when spending. It will also teach you to keep track of every penny spent so you can be true to your budget. Take control of these expenses—this is where the devil lives.

Discretionary Monthly Expenses Worksheet

Monthly Expenses	Current Monthly Payment	Adjusted to Balance Income
Recreation/Member Dues	$	$
Children's Dues and Club Fees	$	$
Movie and Game Rentals	$	$
Concerts	$	$
Movies/Plays	$	$
Dining Out	$	$
Sporting Events	$	$
Magazines/Newspapers	$	$
Self-Care (dermatology, therapy, and so on)	$	$
Barber/Beauty Salon	$	$
Hobbies	$	$
Fundraisers/Dues	$	$
Other	$	$
Other	$	$
Other	$	$
Total Monthly Discretionary Expenses	$	$

Before moving on to the next section, allow me to tell you a quick story that illustrates my point. I was instructing a husband and wife, in their late thirties, on how to craft a budget but the numbers never seemed to work. The money that they brought in and the money they spent didn't make sense to me. According to the numbers, they should have had no problems making ends meet. Something was wrong, because there wasn't more money left over each month. Both of them swore that they were being sincere. Their marriage appeared to be open, honest, and healthy. They appeared to be a loving couple, but their money woes were beginning to put a strain on their relationship—and here's why.

Let's start with the husband. Every week he and the guys would go out for Buffalo wings, pizza, beer, and some pool. Whenever the guys made plans he'd tell his wife that he was working late that evening—a little white lie he justified by convincing himself that he couldn't let the guys down. The problem was that he never accounted for that money. He believed that he deserved some time with the guys and that money was his to spend. By the time he was finished he usually ended up spending around $35, depending on how much he lost in pool, because there was always a friendly wager involved. He failed to recognize that he was not only lying to his wife but was also spending $140 a month or more.

Now it's the wife's turn. Even though they both promised to pack their lunches each day to save money, she still went out to lunch twice a week at work. The husband never noticed because he left earlier than her each morning and thought that she would pack a lunch after he was gone. After a while he forgot all about it. Well, at approximately $10 per lunch she was spending $20 per week or $80 a month.

When we total these indulgences, the amounts come to nearly $220 per month; on an annual basis the amount totals $2,640. Now we are talking serious money. That's a lot of money when you are having a difficult time paying your bills. When they finally admitted their indiscretions to each other, they were disappointed in themselves and each other. They had emotionally and financially betrayed each other after they both promised to change their spending habits. It was not a pretty scene, but I'm happy to report that they changed their ways. The husband still goes out with the guys but only once a month and she rarely buys lunch anymore. They finally realized that their finances, especially their discretionary spending, were an important aspect of their lives and their marriage. They needed more than ever to be a team, to assist each other and be open about their spending. This was a hard lesson, but a lesson that each could learn not only about tracking expenses but also about being completely honest and forthright.

Time to Calculate

Okay, let's say that you are done gathering all of your income and expenses and entering them into the budgeting worksheets. Now take your total expenses and subtract them from the total income figure for the month. Then divide your total expenses by the number of paychecks you (and your spouse) receive each month. This number is the amount you should set aside each paycheck. If your expense total is more than your income total, we have some serious work to do.

For example:

Total Fixed Monthly Expenses: $2,500
Total Flexible Monthly Expenses: $500
Total Discretionary Monthly Expenses: $200
Total Monthly Expenses are $3,200 less Income of $4,000
    = $800 per month surplus
Number of Monthly Paychecks = 4
Total Expenses of $3,200 divided by number of Monthly
    Paychecks of 4 = $800

In this example you would need to allocate $800 per paycheck for expenses. This lets you know that you have $200 per check to put for emergency savings, your retirement plan, or a specific goal.

The work starts here and it's also where the fun begins; start making sacrifices if your budget is off. Get it into your mind that change is necessary, and you will succeed. Like I said, you will discover many things about yourself and others as you make progress. I will be with you every step of the way. Okay, let's learn some more about saving money and altering your spending habits.

The Frugal Philosophy

Now that you have a better understanding of how to craft a budget, let me help you become frugal. Some people criticize those of us who try to be frugal. They are simply confusing frugality with being cheap. When you hear the word *cheap*, it grates on your eardrums. No one likes a cheapskate. We've all been programmed to think of someone who is out to save a buck or two as being cheap. Say the word out loud; it's annoying—a quick one-syllable word that more often than not evokes emotions that tilt toward disgust. I'm not talking about being cheap. I'm talking about being smart. I'm talking about embracing the frugal philosophy. The dictionary gives us the meaning of frugal: *characterized by or reflecting economy in the use of resources.*

It's really quite beautiful—economy in the use of resources. Let's say that again, but with one word added: Economy in the use of *your* resources. Think of a great Italian chef preparing a marinara sauce for a special dinner. Do you think the chef is going to be extravagant, adding layer after layer of ingredients until his marinara sauce has lost its true character? No. The chef will use simple, fresh ingredients: tomatoes, garlic, basil, olive oil, salt, and pepper. He will coax a magnificent aroma and flavor out of an economy of resources. He's not being cheap; he's being true to the nature of things. Simple is better, in the art of cooking and in the world of finances. Sure, there are times when something complicated can be rewarding, but there is nothing more breathtaking than simplicity raised to the highest levels. That's what we are after when I say start being frugal. Embrace the word *frugality*. Love the word *frugality*. Feel the word *frugality*. Become the word *frugality*.

Since we are on the subject of food, let's start at the grocery store because we all need to eat and a substantial portion of our take-home pay goes toward food. I talked about shopping earlier, but let's get more serious. Shopping for groceries does not begin in the grocery store; it begins in your home, specifically at your kitchen table. Yes, coupon cutting is wise (if that's what first popped into your head) and it can save money, but the true philosophy of saving money when buying food starts with the list. Your list should not be a hodgepodge of items that you need to replenish, nor should it be a bunch of items that are on sale. Base your list on meals—think breakfast, lunch, and dinner for your family, whether it's five people or just you.

Think of the week ahead and buy accordingly. Let's say you shop on Saturday or Sunday, but it really doesn't matter. Plan your dinner meals first; Monday is pasta night, Tuesday meat and vegetables, Wednesday BLT sandwiches with a tossed salad, and so forth. This way you will know exactly what to buy, but don't drill down to one type of meat, like chicken on Tuesday, because you may get to the store and find that it is having a sale on beef. Maintaining a certain amount of flexibility allows you to save money.

Most people don't plan their meals, and they stand there at the meat counter and contemplate what they are going to eat, all the while wasting their time and crowding the aisle. You'll learn that being prepared and being frugal is smart. Not only will you save money, but time as well. How many times have you been in the grocery store and witnessed people walking aimlessly? It seems as though they've never seen a banana or a box of cereal before. I admit that I have done that—pushing my cart around the displays of apples, pears, oranges, and strawberries wondering what the heck am I going to buy. Do you know what that activity leads to—spending more money and wasting a lot of brain power and time. If you don't have a list, you'll end up buying things you don't need and forgetting the items you do need. It's a double whammy. You waste money and you waste time because when you arrive back at your home, you'll realize that you forgot a few things and then you're back in the car heading for the store all over again. Chances are that you'll spend even more money because you'll end up buying other things that you stumble across. With a list that headache is gone. You have a list and on that list it says fruit for snacks and lunches. You find the fruit that is on sale, if not on sale then reasonably priced, and you place it in your cart and move on.

When I talk about the frugal philosophy and contemplating the economy of resources used, I'm not only talking about money, I am also talking about time. We also "spend" time. Who wants to spend all of their time in a busy grocery store? Not me. I also don't want my wife or me to spend too much time cooking during the week. Let's face it: it's a hassle and most people are tired when they get home from work. So we plan meals that are inexpensive, easy to make, and nutritious. Think pasta tossed with fresh vegetables and topped with a little cheese. That takes 20 minutes to prepare and everyone is happy. I can also use the leftover vegetables in a soup or an omelet. Don't ever forget to reuse your leftovers. You have chicken from the night before? Chop it up, open a can of kidney beans, warm up the chicken and beans, and make tacos or burritos—think ahead, be smart, proactive and always be frugal.

Now, moving toward breakfast, the most important meal of the day: I want something quick and easy—breakfast cereal. Most cereals, hot or cold, have a robust amount of nutrition per serving. But, and this is important, many of those cereals have too much sugar or high-fructose corn syrup in them. Read the labels and determine which cereal has a good portion of protein and fiber compared to sugar. You not only want to be frugal, but you also want to be healthy. Most supermarkets have at least half a dozen cereals on sale every time you go to the store. Many times there are two-for-one deals, which is even better. Choose to eat cereal because it not only tastes good, but it also is nutritious—and you only need to add milk. It's easy and it saves time. You can usually find milk on sale, too. Cereal can be eaten at any meal.

Lunch is a bit trickier. If you have kids going to school or a spouse who need lunches packed, you will have to really get creative—and that's part of the fun! Most people like to pack sandwiches with a snack or two and a drink. I'll use my two nephews as an example. Kids get a sandwich, two snacks (one of the snacks is a piece of fruit), and a drink. Look for lunch meat that is on sale or keep peanut butter and jelly in the house. That's a good staple and relatively healthy. You can usually find two-for-one loaves of bread and a variety of juices on sale. Never skimp on nutrition—look for whole-wheat bread or whole-grain breads and juices with less sugar.

We've just skimmed the surface of being frugal when it comes to food shopping. You will want to carry this philosophy over to every aspect of your life if possible. Let me give you an example from a client of mine. She ran into a perfect storm, if you will, of bad financial luck: She was laid off of work and was overwhelmed by medical bills as a result of an accident her child experienced. She basically lost everything but was determined and most certainly galvanized by the thought of getting her financial privileges back. She found another job and immediately gathered other employees who lived near her neighborhood. She asked them if they were interested in carpooling. Most said no, but a few agreed and now she drives her car to work only twice a week, saving money on gas and wear and tear. What really excited me was her effort: She brought evidence, showing her coworkers how much money they could save on gas if they joined her carpool. She did the work. But what also shocked me was that most people said no. They didn't care about saving money. They couldn't see the value of being frugal even when they were staring at it. Some people don't want to be obligated to other people's schedules. Some people need the alone time to relax and unwind. Some are anti-social. I understand it. I'm all three sometimes. That being said, if you have money problems you need to change your spending habits and maybe some personal habits. This is one way.

This client also makes a very detailed shopping list and sticks to it, and she stops every Sunday at an organic farm that allows customers to pick their own fruits and vegetables. She not only gets exercise and spends time with her kids, but she also is saving a bunch of money while gathering food that is nutritious and tastes great. Her previous routine of buying coffee every morning has been replaced by drinking coffee at home from a coffee maker she found at a yard sale for $3—and it was still in the box, not used. Once or twice a month she and the family go to a pizzeria that offers large pizzas for $7.99. It feeds everyone and they all order water with lemon so as not to incur an extra expense—soft drinks and alco-holic drinks are usually outrageously priced compared to what it actually costs to make or buy from the wholesaler. Those extra savings allow them to give the waiter or wait-ress a slightly higher tip. The wait staff always remembers them, and their service reflects it. You see, she is not being cheap; she is being smart and frugal.

Her kids wear basic uniforms to school—a white or blue collared shirt with khaki shorts or a skirt. She found a store that discounted these types of clothing because they wanted the business of the parents whose kids attended that school. The parent-teachers association at the school holds a used uniform sale each year at prices that are 10 percent of what new uniforms would cost. She bought in bulk and saved a bundle. She has learned that using a certain detergent for washing her clothes gives her six more loads of wash compared to the other brands she bought, and teaching her kids to turn out the lights and turn off the TV and computer when they are not being used saves money. She even sits her kids down and shows them the difference in the bills each month, which encourages the kids to help out even more. More importantly, she is actually involving her children in family finances which will have tremendous benefits now and certainly in the future when the children have to run their own household budget. This single act qualifies her for my Parental Honor Roll as it will, in my opinion, positively impact her children's lives. No parent wants to see their children struggle. If you teach them early how to avoid financial hardship, they may not experience it later in life.

I think, in the end, the frugal philosophy can become contagious. It's intelligent but it's also a difficult philosophy to adopt and sustain because we've all been programmed to spend. We are being brainwashed daily by television ads, in-your-face radio commercials in which people scream about outrageous savings on new cars, and

Internet popups and store banners that promulgate "the sale of all sales!" It never ends, but it doesn't have to be that way. Take aim at them and fire back. Be frugal and get more for your money and more for your family. You'll be happier and have a few extra bucks in your savings account to show for it.

Chapter THREE

Discovering a New Outlook on Life and Money

During the adventure of becoming empowered you will discover new outlooks and perspectives about the world around you. Taking back your financial power and challenging yourself forces you to look deep inside, to question your beliefs and the things that you have been doing, to realize that your actions have impacted you and perhaps the people around you, like your family. Many people call this discovery an epiphany—a powerful spiritual awakening.

The awakening happens to characters in the movies and in books and it happens to real people every day. It usually occurs when a person is desperate and hits rock bottom, like when an alcoholic wakes up one morning and realizes that he has lost everything—his family has left him, he has no friends, and he is utterly alone. He then suddenly understands that he must do something to change his life or perish. It could be more mundane, like when people decide to switch careers because something they did or experienced touched them so deeply that they had no choice. I read about a 45-year-old man who went scuba diving for the first time and when he saw the beautiful world beneath the sea it nearly brought him to tears. It changed him and now, five years later, he's an underwater photographer.

An awakening can happen to you—it may not be as dramatic, but who knows? You have experienced a life-altering event. Losing your financial independence, no matter what the reason is, can act like a catalyst, propelling you toward a whole new outlook on life—physically, emotionally, and spiritually. It could also ruin you, sending you on a free fall of self-pity and anger. We're not going to let that happen. We're traveling together toward an awakening that instills confidence and empowers you to make extraordinary changes and experience extraordinary results.

Identify Your Values: Work, Friends, and Family

Let's start by identifying your values—what's most important to you. Let's face it, there are many people in this world that care more about material possessions, such as their mint-condition Mustang or a wardrobe, than they do about the truly important things in life, like family and friends. That's one reason why people get themselves into crises: They don't have their values in order. They fail to recognize the true meaning of life. They fail to cherish the important aspects we are all granted. Now, I don't want to come off as a preacher and I'm not a therapist (although those close to me will tell you I need one); if you don't agree with what I have to say, that's your prerogative. I am here to help you with your financial situation, and in my opinion—and I have been in the debt-counseling and financial arena for many years and have personally counseled tens of thousands of families—examining and dissecting your values is imperative especially when it comes to spending and saving money.

We'll begin with the work you do. A high percent-age of people in America don't enjoy their jobs. They do the job simply because they get paid. They don't find any enjoyment, excitement, or challenges day to day, and that's not healthy. If you seriously hate your work, you should try in earnest to find another occupation. I know it's easier said than done, but it has been done many times before so there's no reason to lose hope. You will never be successful unless you love what you're doing. A life without passion is not a life. A career without satisfac-tion is not a career.

Being miserable for most of your day and not mak-ing the income you think you're worth obviously influ-ences the way you feel about yourself and probably the way you feel about those around you. A very wise man once told me that if you're happy at work, you're happy at home. He went on to say that if you're happy at home everything else around you falls into place. You might be envious of others because they enjoy their jobs or have a perceived higher income. Some people who make excel-lent money, though, also hate their jobs, but they've usu-ally created a certain expensive lifestyle that gives them a measure of joy but that also prevents them from finding a job that they love. More times than not, the job they would love to do pays a whole lot less. So it works at both ends of the spectrum.

Here's where the value of work comes into play. At the beginning of the last paragraph I said that you might be unhappy because you're "not making the income you think you're worth." I can't remember how many times I've heard people utter that phrase. I've felt it before, too. The thing is we all have to prove our worth or find a job that carries so much personal value that it's worth doing regardless of the pay. Of course there is no shortage of bad employers who don't care how hard you work for them; they just want more from you but won't pay for it. It's not fair, but fairness has nothing to do with it. Getting frustrated and angry over it is just a waste of time, and your time has value and that's what we're after.

So now after all the financial turmoil you have an opportunity to start over, and please, treat this as an opportunity, as a second chance. Ask yourself this question: How will I get the most value out of my work? I have come across a variety of answers, but I can't answer that question for you; you have to figure out what you want from your work. I can give you an example of how a group of people found value at work, or thought they found value and, to some extent, how that value was a reflection of their lives.

In my younger years I was friends with some guys who sold cars. They were an ambitious bunch ranging from their early twenties to their mid-thirties. They liked to say that they worked hard and played hard. They found value in the money they made selling cars and the things they bought with that money. Many of these guys were ex-athletes, so they enjoyed the competition of who could sell more cars per month. They worked insane hours, usually arriving at the dealership around eight in the morning and not leaving until 10 or 11 that night. I don't know if you have ever sold cars, but it can be terribly boring. Hours can go by without talking with one customer, so the managers want the salesmen on the phone trying to drum up business from customers who visited but did not buy. So when a salesman does get a customer who seems even vaguely interested in a car, the salesman is supposed to seal the deal. After all, it's about getting the cars off the lot, not about pleasing the customer. These guys would use every trick in the book to get someone to buy or lease a car.

The thing is, they found satisfaction in convincing people to buy, even if the buyers couldn't afford the car. It's how they got paid. It was a game to them. Many people wouldn't be able to sleep at night knowing that they sold something to a person who couldn't afford it. That's sales for you. These guys would joke about it while spending their commission on round after round of drinks. They certainly worked hard and played hard.

While hanging out with these guys on occasion I noticed that after six months or so they would be working at a new dealership. It was crazy. They would get laid off from one place and start at another the next week. It was a vicious cycle; they had to sell, sell, and sell. I also noticed as time passed the job wore them down and they became more and more callous toward customers. The only time these guys were happy was when they were partying; otherwise they were either sleeping or at work.

For more than half of these guys, the value slowly faded. Sure, they could make money but they didn't have a life. They couldn't enjoy the other valuable things that the world offered. A few guys were married and had kids. They could pay the bills, but the pressure to sell was overbearing and they rarely saw their kids, even on Sunday. Many years later I talked with one of the guys in that group. Only two of them were still selling cars. The rest of them either went back to school so they could find a better job or found other work that provided more value than just a commission check. He also said that he thought the work was not a proper reflection of who he was. That's not to say all car salespeople are bad or have no conscience, but it does take a certain personality to get the job done. He works as a nurse in a hospice now. He makes less money but he loves his work. It's a far cry from hustling cars.

In the end, it's up to you—would you like your own cubicle where you can hang a few favorite pictures or would you rather be outside? Maybe you enjoy working on computers in an office, or maybe you'd rather be going from business to business selling specialized products. You might want to start a business selling unique pottery—who knows, but if it brings you joy and you can make money then give it a try. Otherwise it's just a hobby. We do want to find value, but the bottom line will always be that you have to earn a paycheck. So if you are unhappy at work, then plan to change. You may not be able to change right away, or you may not want to change at all.

That's fine. If you are happy at work then you are one of the lucky people and you are free to start focusing on the other items in life that bring value and joy.

It's good to have friends. The right kind of friends add value to your life by picking you up when you're feeling down, by being there when you need them, and very good friends are in a unique position to sit you down and tell you when you're screwing up. Friends can also help you regain your financial independence, not by lending you money but by offering support and understanding as you discover your financial power. Good friends understand that you're not in a position to go out every weekend. They understand and appreciate your company more than the peripheral excitement of a nightclub or happy hour or any other type of entertainment that you may not be able to afford right now.

Unlike associates, acquaintances, or colleagues, you don't or shouldn't feel the urge to compete with your friends or keep up with them in certain aspects of your life—like your financial life. For example, if your friend purchases a vehicle or a luxury item such as a boat, you should feel happy for them—and vice versa. That's what separates true friends from everyone else. Many people have a hard time watching other people succeed, and some people who succeed can't be bothered with the "friends" they had before they achieved a certain status level. Sometimes one factor can ruin a friendship, and it's usually money. Sometimes that feeling is reversed. Feelings of inadequacy may hibernate for years. Most of those times, it's unfounded and just in the imagination of one party.

So here you are in a financial crisis, trying to start over again. Now is the time to take a good look around to see which friends are sticking close to you. I have a friend from high school whose father owned a small business in the town we grew up in. The Petersons weren't wealthy but they were comfortable. The business flourished for a while and Mr. Peterson had a lot of friends and colleagues—they went to dinner together, parties, they were on the same bowling team, and their wives were all friends too.

Eventually the business failed, mostly because of personal reasons. The Peterson family went from a four-bedroom home with all the amenities, including two very nice cars in the driveway, to a small rental home in a bad part of town in a matter of weeks. My friend and his two brothers shared a bedroom, and the entire family shared one bathroom, which made it nearly impossible for everyone to get ready for school and work in the morning. It was a sad scene, but they made the best of a bad situation.

Remember when I said Mr. Peterson had a lot of friends and colleagues? Well, the majority of those "friends" disappeared when he was no longer a part of that social scene. No one had time for him or, more likely, they didn't feel comfortable around him, especially since he could not partake in their usual escapades, which entailed spending money. One day another friend of mine and his father were driving home from the store and they both noticed Mr. Peterson standing by his car on the side of the road holding a gas can. Mr. Peterson apparently had run out of gas and was getting ready to walk four or five miles to the gas station. My friend's father pulled over and offered Mr. Peterson a lift. After an uncomfortable silence Mr. Peterson said okay and got into the car.

On the way to the gas station no one said a word. As my friend recalled the story, they arrived at the gas station and Mr. Peterson got out of the car and waited for the attendant. When the attendant arrived he asked for 67 cents' worth of gas. Gas was probably only about 50 cents a gallon then. He remembers that number (67) because he thinks that was all the money Mr. Peterson had in his pocket. They drove back to Mr. Peterson's car in silence again, and when they arrived Mr. Peterson got out of the car. He stood next to the car for a few seconds and then reached in through the open window to shake my friend's father's hand. He said "thank you" and then turned away. When they drove away, my friend's father turned to him and said, "He may not have the business or the same money that he once had, but he's still the same man."

My friend's father was right. Even though Mr. Peterson lost everything and was struggling, he was still the same man. I want you to think about that. I realize that immediately after a crisis you feel changed because of it—but you are still that same person deep down inside. Those friends that are closest to you will understand that fact. You the person are more valuable to them, and in return you also receive value because of their devotion. You may act more stressed and feel burdened by your financial misfortunes, but don't be too rough on yourself. Learn from the crisis and become a stronger, smarter person. If you've noticed that some people you thought were friends no longer return your calls or come around, then so be it. You're better off. They probably weren't your friends to begin with.

I once had a very difficult time; it wasn't financial but it was serious just the same. When news of my difficulties became public, most of the people who I thought were my close friends had my back. Some just inquired if I was okay, and all except one gave me support. The one who did not come to my emotional aid ran away from me as far as he could, and at the height of the situation essentially denounced our friendship. Obviously that friendship ended on a very bad note. He still calls me from time to time and wonders why I don't want anything to do with him.

Friends you can trust are more of a luxury than anything you could possibly buy or own. I can't even begin to remember all the wonderful stories my clients have told me about how their friends helped them pull through the tough times. They would have collapsed under the pressure of their financial calamities if it weren't for the friends who helped them bear the weight.

Now it's time to discuss family. It's a cliché, but we've all heard the expression "Family comes first." Many people believe that, and it would be a pleasant world if that were true, but let's not be too naïve. We as humans can be caring, but we can also be incredibly selfish. Let's use my neighbor as an example—the man who bought the dirt bike for his son in Chapter 1. At face value, it seemed like he wanted to please his son, do anything for the boy to make him happy, even if the consequences would harm him. He's putting his son's happiness first—family first. But that's not the truth, even if he talked himself into it, reasoned it out in his head: "I'm going to do everything I can to make my son happy. He deserves it, and just because his mother and I are getting a divorce it doesn't mean he should suffer."

This father, like many other parents and adults, moved forward without truly contemplating the results of his selfish actions. I say selfish because the dirt bike was really purchased because the father suffered from guilt, and he believed that the only way to ease those feelings was to buy something for his boy. He was thinking of himself, not his son. We know the outcome: The dirt bike was finally taken by the bank because the father couldn't afford it in the first place. So what are the final results? More guilt, and now it's compounded by humiliation and shame. It's going to take a man's effort on the boy's part to figure out what the heck just happened. Was his father being stupid? Was he trying to show his mother up? How will he explain the loss of the dirt bike to his friends? These questions become like an unruly mob in the poor kid's head. The upside is that a lesson can be learned from this event—the father can use it to teach his child about finances. It's a lesson that the child can use the rest of his life. Now I'm not suggesting that anyone should pur-posely put themselves in financial dire straits, but I am telling you that if you are or were in this type of situation, get some benefit from it. Teach your kids what not to do by example.

Back to the story, you can see the dilemma. By not clearly thinking through the financial consequences, the adult made a bad situation worse for his family. A similar situation could have just as easily happened in a home where two happily married adults lived with their children. Let's say these two adults spent beyond their means—nice cars, a beautiful home, and a pool. The material posses-sions have become the focus and not the family. The two adults may think that the material things are a reflection of their family values or how much they love their kids and each other, but if they took a moment to step out-side of themselves and really consider their situation they could possibly experience an epiphany. That is extremely difficult for most people and they usually have to force the moment to its crisis before they realize change is needed. So let's do it for them. What if we take everything away, the cars, the house, the neighborhood, the pool, everything? They are now left with each other.

When families are put into these situations they usu-ally understand very quickly how much they value each other. If they are forced to move into an apartment or smaller home, then they can't run away from each other like they could in a large home or drive off because they may only have one car in the family now. They are forced to confront one another and the emotions can be raw. The kids may feel betrayed and the adults may feel foolish. That's why it's so important to build a foundation that starts with family values. It's not the money made or the money spent, it's not the cars, the clothes, and all the peripheral luxuries—it's the family. Place your value in your family. If you live alone or don't have much of a family you're close with, then place it in yourself; respect yourself. When the opulence disappears, the only things left are the people. The values of a family manifest themselves in the use of teamwork; it's the job of picking one another up, supporting one another through the good times and the bad.

Think of it like this: You may have loved your car or your house and the things in it; you may have loved the neighborhood you lived in, the variety of clothes you had, and the freedom, real or imagined, to spend money when you felt like it. Those *things* didn't love you back; no matter how you lost them or what the circumstances were, they did not love you back. That's what family members and friends do—they love you back regardless of the financial situation. They give you the energy to fight and the inspiration to help you achieve your goals.

The Value of Money

During my time in the debt consolidation and credit-counseling industry, I've noticed a trend—too many people don't value money. Unfortunately this is not surprising.

Take yourself as an example. You may have lost everything and there are a multitude of reasons why this might have happened—overspending, loss of a job, a sudden sickness—and you weren't sufficiently prepared for the fallout. Here's the kicker: For the most part it's not your fault due to the society we live in and the marketing we are all exposed to; you've been programmed to think of the value of money in a way much different from your grandparents or great-grandparents. They, for the most part, actually valued each dollar saved and spent. We as a society don't do that. How many times have you heard phrases such as "As soon as I get my money it's already spent" or "I don't know where all the money goes"?

Those phrases seem trivial because day-to-day, pay-check-to-paycheck living is the norm. Not many people have the luxury of saving even a minimal portion of their paycheck because they have bills to pay and because they spend their money on frivolous items. You'll probably notice some frivolous items of your own when you create your budget. If you don't place value on your money, then you simply don't respect your money and that can lead to financial misfortunes. Even if you didn't overspend and say, you suffered an unfortunate health issue and couldn't afford the doctor bills, how much money did you have in your emergency fund? These are tough questions to answer. Maybe you had some money, maybe not much at all. The point is that saving money is not a priority for most people, and if bad luck strikes they have nowhere to turn.

So why do so many people overspend? One of the problems is credit cards. They're not money; they don't look like money or feel like money and when you purchase an item with a credit card you don't get that nauseating feeling of spending a large amount of cash. Take a look at all the credit card commercials—everyone is smiling and it's simply joyous. Why? Because the credit card is helping you purchase a dream, or because when you use your credit card you are getting money back or getting some reward in return. It's brilliant. Spend a bunch of money that you probably don't have and we'll give you a small fraction of that money back. It's a deal that you can't afford not to take—even if you can't afford it. At least, that's what the lenders want you to think.

Every day mailboxes all around the country are filled with 0 percent financing offers and other such promises from credit card marketers and whoever else. Just fill in the blanks, and they'll do the rest. It's not reality. It's an illusion, a message that plays right into the American psyche. We want things, and we want them now. There's no better way to get what you want—a new flat screen, shoes, stereo, a lavish night on the town—than with a credit card. You're not parting with cash; you're simply signing a piece of paper and you get the credit card back! You didn't lose a thing. You leave with your new stuff and you still have your credit card. What a deal, except when the bill comes in.

How could you possibly find value in that version of reality? If you paid cash for everything then you would understand and appreciate the value of money. Think about what it would take to save $1,000 for an item you really want. A lot of time and effort would be invested before you could finally purchase that item. The purchase would feel like an accomplishment. It doesn't feel that way with a credit card. You don't achieve that sense of satisfaction; there is no triumph. There is the instant gratification and then the feeling of sheer doom when you receive the credit card bill.

I understand that it's hard to pay cash for everything and not use a credit card, but it's not impossible. I think if you figure out your needs and wants you'd be surprised at how far your cash could go. Of course that means sacrifice. You may not be able to have every movie channel on your cable or satellite TV (do you really need 500 channels?), but when you get down to it, when you seriously focus on value you'll realize what's important and what's insignificant.

The Value of Living for Tomorrow

How about some more phrases to think about—*live for today, tomorrow may never come; live every day like it's your last*. These sayings make great movie lines but they aren't realistic. At a primal level I think we would all like to live every day like it's our last, but that's probably not a good idea, at least in the way that many people comprehend those words. For me living every day like it's your last means being happy, appreciative of what you have, and thankful for your family and friends and for those few materialistic things that bring some joy to your life. That's not easy to do. Things get in the way and ruin your good mood, making you frustrated and angry. Little day-to-day dilemmas can really mess things up.

As a result of those day-to-day quandaries, or for other reasons or frustrations, I think some people take those phrases too literally. It's true, this could be your last day on earth and that's a scary feeling, but that doesn't mean you should do something financially irresponsible. What happens when you wake up the next day after doing something financially foolish? You're still here, except now you must face the consequences of your misguided decisions. It may seem ludicrous, but some people think that "Hey, I might not be here tomorrow or next week, so I'm going to enjoy myself now!" That enjoyment is almost always associated with spending lots of money—money they don't have. There is no value in that philosophy because there's a better than good chance that they'll be around when the credit card bill arrives.

This has become a part of our culture. It's a "now or never" belief system that's not healthy, especially when you are talking in financial terms. When speaking about finances, you are always looking toward the future. You plan so that bills can be paid, so that there are extra funds for an emergency, and you propose strategies so that one day you can retire. The "instant gratification" and "living for today" model runs counter to those values.

The value of living for tomorrow provides you and your family with security, hope, and opportunity. You can think of security in terms of savings in the bank or investments in stocks and bonds. If something breaks down and you need cash in a hurry it's there for you, and the stocks and bonds are securing your future. Hope is found in the belief that you and your family will be able to overcome financial obstacles and you won't have to go through the devastating physical and emotional tribulations inherent in bankruptcy and other forms of financial failure. When you value money and you live for tomorrow, opportunity abounds—your kids have the chance to attend college, you can retire one day, or you may simply be able to purchase something without worrying if you can afford it.

You are on a journey of financial power, so you are living for tomorrow, living for a very different future. If you have a set of values that assist you rather than hinder you, then reaching your goal won't be as difficult. If you value your work, friends, and family then you will have those three things as powerful allies. If you learn the value of money then you will be more educated when it comes to spending, saving, and using credit cards. It's not an easy road; a crisis can be waiting around any bend. If you continue to believe in yourself and focus on what I'm teaching you, then success is waiting, tomorrow is waiting, and that in itself is valuable.

Chapter FOUR

Staying on the Right Path

We've covered a myriad of topics so far, and I hope you are getting a feel for how to regain your focus and confidence when dealing with financial matters and perhaps with your personal outlook on life. As you can see, financial recovery is based sometimes on numbers and sometimes on psychology. Now you want to put those things in motion, applying them to your everyday actions. This may not be easy, especially when we are greeted daily by the "spend" mentality of our society. I can give you an example. Just the other day I received a catalogue from a cookware company. The first five pages alone had a slew of specialty items that would supposedly make life easier in the kitchen and also allow you to cook wonderful dishes for your family. We're talking omelet pans, pancake makers, indoor grills and fryers, meshed grill pans, jalapeño pepper roasters, electric rotisserie items, margarita makers, and an assortment of waffle makers, blenders, juicers, slicers, graters, and peelers. I could go on. Funny thing is, when I cook I'm not that extravagant. Give me a pot, a pan, and a couple of simple utensils and I'm off to the races.

Are some of these items useful, even cool? Yes. But do you really need to spend $20 on a tomato slicer? I would say no. You can use a knife. Also, think about storage. Where on earth are you going to put all of these gadgets? An associate of mine loves these types of things.

She collects them, but when it comes time to use one of them it usually takes 15 minutes to find, and then I have to laugh because the item is rarely in good shape—it's a bit dirty or a piece is missing. She doesn't have the proper storage or the time to maintain these revolutionary devices. In the end, a lot of these items end up in garage sales selling for a few dimes or a quarter. It's a waste.

If you are honest with yourself you will realize that you don't need those types of possessions; what you do need is to focus on building up your financial foundation. Why even tempt yourself? Cancel the catalogues or just throw them away without even opening them. Separate yourself from that "spend" mindset. Now let's go a step further and investigate a few ideas on how to stay on the right path.

Find a Hobby

A hobby is an inexpensive and stimulating method for saving money and expanding your horizons. I've had clients who took up knitting, fishing, writing, reading, sewing, furniture refinishing, and other creative activities, which granted them joy and a sense of accomplishment without their having to spend much money. The idea is to stay away from the places or things that switch on your "spend motor."

Many people I deal with complain about being bored or not satisfied with their day-to-day life. So in order to generate some excitement they go shopping or find some other pursuit that usually involves spending money they don't have—going to a restaurant or a movie. In fact, I see a ton of people go shopping just to pass the time, but that's wasting time and it can cost hundreds of dollars per hour. We want to save money and fill up your empty time with inspiring, educational, and purpose-packed activities. We want to avoid the afternoons at the mall because other than being with your friends or family members (unless you go alone) there is no payback; you only pay out. When I say "payback" I mean getting reimbursed in a very satisfying manner after you accomplish what you set out to do. "Pay out" refers to your spending and the fact that you are only getting satisfied at one level—a materialistic level after purchasing an item, which doesn't last long.

Let me give you a few examples of people who found hobbies that actually improved their outlook on life, their health, their attitude, and their financial condition. These hobbies provided them with a payback they never experienced before. I want to point out one other thing first: Even if you didn't hit rock bottom because of spending, hobbies are a wonderful option for saving more money. You have spare time so why not fill it with something that won't create an additional expense.

A single, middle-aged client used to stop off at a bar after work to have a few drinks, enjoy the happy hour company (all the regulars knew his name), and maybe get a bite to eat. He didn't always have the cash to spend, so he would put it on his credit card. In his mind, he was actually saving money because he was there at happy hour and the drink prices were reduced. It's funny how you can easily persuade yourself into believing something that's not really true. Sure, the drink prices were reduced, but he was still paying something and the meals were not cheap, and he left a nice tip. When I spoke with him at length about spending and saving money and creating a budget, he really didn't want to give up his happy hour. He told me that he got lonely at home and the company there was nice. I also found out that he would frequent the mall and take walks down town on the weekends just to be around people. The problem, though, was he didn't have the extra cash to go to the mall and when he went downtown he would inevitably eat lunch in a restaurant. So each time he wanted company it cost him money that he didn't have. So not only did this client partake in the unhealthy activity of drinking and eating out followed by shopping for items he didn't need, but he also adopted a method of passing time that was unhealthy for his wallet.

It's tough to delve into people's personal lives, but if I don't find out where and why they are spending their money I can't help them. There is another point here that is important—the man was honest with me and with himself. It wasn't easy for him to admit that he was lonely. Those people at the bar were nice to say hello to and maybe chat for a bit but they weren't friends. They didn't have much in common, except that they liked booze! So I asked what his interests were. Did he have any hobbies or a passion for something? It turned out that he used to make model cars and he loved to spend hour after hour making certain every intricate part fit perfectly. He also enjoyed painting them after they were complete. Once he told me that I grabbed the Yellow Pages and looked up *hobbies* and found a place that sold model cars not far from his house. There was still a problem, though; he built these model cars alone. I told him that there must be other people who shared his passion; all he had to do was find them. It turned out that there was a club he could join at the hobby shop—a model-making club. It was perfect. He joined the club and they met a couple times a week to share thoughts and tips on model making and to show off the cars that they completed. They even shared glue, paints, brushes, and other necessities to cut down on the cost of completing a model. It turned out that some other people involved were trying to save money. That's a win-win situation. Listen, I know that model making isn't everyone's cup of tea, but it helped him meet people and find friendship, and it saved him money. When we got done creating his budget, the nights at the bar were cut from his discretionary expenses. That was no small victory for him; it was a monumental triumph.

I work with a lot of couples, husbands and wives who, little by little, loosened the grip on their spending or suffered a job loss or another financial crisis and couldn't maintain the frantic pace of bill paying. Regardless of how it happens, these couples find themselves in a mineshaft that's about to collapse from the weight of their financial burdens. It's scary, as you very well can imagine. In the case of one couple, the wife lost her job and she was the main bread winner. They had established a certain lifestyle and their oldest son was in college. They needed to drastically cut spending. Some things needed to end immediately—frequenting restaurants for lunch and dinner, premium cable channels, gym memberships that they rarely used, and other basically frivolous expenses. Once we cut everything to a bare minimum, they looked at me and said: "What are we going to do with ourselves?" That's a legitimate question, and it leads to why you should not associate busying yourself with spending money. Here's an example: At least once a month they would rent a boat for half a day at $300. They enjoyed the water and the freedom. I suggested that they rent a canoe at a state park for a small fraction of that cost, or pack a snack and visit the park and enjoy the weather instead of going to a restaurant and spending $60 or $70 for lunch.

We discussed the things that they enjoyed and came to the conclusion that they liked the outdoors and they also wanted to get in better physical condition. What's better than saving tons of money while getting into better condition? The couple was in decent shape but they wanted to improve without too much exertion. I told them that they could walk a few miles a day or maybe less to begin with, and maybe do some light weightlifting. They didn't have to join a gym because the park offered walking trails and they had a few dumbbells that were gathering dust in the closet. The couple also started canoeing, which is a workout, instead of spending money on a motorboat. They did all this together, so they strengthened not only their bodies but also their relationship. I spoke with them a few months later, and they were happy. They told me that they didn't miss spending all that money and they began to see how foolish it was to pay out and not receive anything worthwhile in return. They started cooking meals together at home, and the husband was becoming a whiz in the kitchen—the stress of spending money that they didn't have was replaced by a sense of fulfillment. The wife found another job; it didn't pay as well but she enjoyed the work. Also, because they decided to get a grip on their spending they didn't need the extra money. They actually were able to keep saving for their retirement!

I want to highlight one thing before we move on. I mentioned that they didn't have to join a gym to get into shape. Gyms are fine if you can afford them, but there are so many other methods for getting into shape if you want to take that up as a hobby. Go to a yard sale or shop that sells used products and you will probably find a workout DVD. You've seen them advertised—cardio workouts, aerobics, weightlifting—you name it and it's available. You may even find a used treadmill, stationary bike, or elliptical machine that's very inexpensive. The thing is you really don't need them. You can walk out your front door and use the world as your treadmill. If you live alone, maybe a neighbor would like to start exercising with you. I see groups of men or women walking all the time. It's a nice way to unwind and ease the strain of your daily life. If you're in a relationship, it's a nice way to spend time together.

Speaking of garage sales, who knows what you may find at a yard sale that could turn into a hobby. Use your imagination. Maybe you'll find a guitar and some old lesson books and just like that you have a hobby. I don't know how many times I've heard clients say that they always wished to learn how to play an instrument. Maybe now is the time. It takes discipline and practice but it's so gratifying—and it's better than using that time to spend money on things that you probably don't need. You should always keep the "reward" factor in mind. When you commit to doing something that may be difficult, like getting back into shape or learning to play the guitar, the reward is so much deeper and the satisfaction at succeeding is uplifting. You don't get that when you are doing things that require spending money. That reward is superficial and fleeting. I like to compare it to people dumping quarters into a slot machine. They get the initial rush, the feeling of hope that swells up inside them, but it soon disappears when they don't win. Or compare it to people who buy a boat but soon realize they can't afford to put gas into it.

For you and the situation you're in now, it's time to find something that brings you joy. You've been through a rough time, and I recommend to all my clients that they pursue a hobby or find a diversion that allows them to free their minds from the worry and stress of their financial crisis. You obviously cannot hide from your dilemma, but it's also not healthy to dwell on it 24 hours a day. Maybe you can coach a baseball team or teach your child or children how to play tennis. There are so many opportunities to improve your financial, physical, and mental well-being. You just need to take advantage of them.

This story is not really about a hobby, but it illustrates what can happen when you decide to use your time in a more productive manner. It's about a young client who lost everything due to a series of bad luck. He, like you, has decided to embark on a journey toward a life where his finances are less tenuous, where he has more control over his money. He decided one day that he was going to fix his car up. It wasn't a new car (probably six or seven years old), but it was his, not the bank's, and he wanted to spruce it up. He purchased some car cleaning products on sale and started from the tires up—washing, waxing, and shining—until the car looked almost new. He then focused his efforts on the inside. He vacuumed the car, cleaned the windows and seats, even scrubbed the nasty stuff off the floorboards with an old toothbrush. He did this over a weekend. One of his neighbors noticed and asked if he could clean her car. She didn't have the time or the gumption to spend hours upon hours refurbishing the car. He thought about it for a while and then decided why not? He had nothing better to do; he could either hang out with a few of his buddies at the beach or make some extra money. So he charged her a flat fee of $75, which included the money he would spend on the products necessary to do the job. He accomplished that task in an afternoon's time and walked away with money in his pocket. The woman told one of her friends about the great job he had done, and the friend told someone and soon my client was cleaning cars on the side. Not a bad way to use up some free time.

A Life without Credit Cards

Learning to live without a credit card is an integral part of financial empowerment. Think of it as a challenge. It may not last forever, but all the lessons you discover will add to your building blocks that will eventually lead to your financial independence.

Considering the position you are in, you may not qualify for a credit card. Believe me, it's not the end of the world, and remember, we are concentrating on how to change your idea of spending and saving money—you are financially reinventing yourself to be stronger, more resilient, and better able to adapt to a fiscal crisis. With that in mind, the Fair Isaac Corporation, the company that produces the FICO credit scoring system, says that 20 million to 25 million people in the United States do not have any credit; further statistics reveal that 30 million to 35 million U.S. residents have a minimal credit history. We don't want to get bogged down in statistics, but that does prove beyond any doubt that there are many people living without credit cards. If my math is correct, those figures amount to 20 percent of all Americans living without credit.

There are several reasons why people don't have credit cards (bad credit, no credit, and so on), but the main point is that they still go about their daily business without laying down that piece of plastic. For them it's all about cash and discipline. Those who don't use credit cards take money much more seriously than credit card users. The act of physically handing over the dollars and cents to a cashier or waitress generates a feeling of loss. That money is gone. When you hand over a credit card there is no money involved, just the plastic; you can worry about that bill later or you may not think about it at all. With tens and twenties, you see it disappearing before your eyes—it's immediate. You know the feeling; you walk out of the house with, say, $53 in your wallet and when you get home you only have $7 left. You count out the $7 and wonder where all your money went, and then you experience that sinking feeling.

Now if you don't use credit cards you will begin to take your money more seriously—at least I hope you do. The first step is to build your savings back up to a healthy point. People with credit cards like to say that they keep them in case of an emergency. Sure, that's fair enough but most of those same people use their credit cards for non-emergencies—those new shoes or those four DVDs did not represent an emergency. You won't have a credit card for an emergency, so you need to set up an emergency fund.

Whether you're paying off debts now or not, you need to start saving. Even just a few dollars a week adds up, but more importantly starting to save money now gets your mind thinking in the right direction. Once you finish liquidating old debts, you take the funds that used to go toward payments and redirect them toward your savings. The rule of thumb about an emergency fund is to accumulate at least six months of your household expenses. This is nice in theory, but it falls short in practicality. When my fellow industry "experts" thought about this they didn't realize they were talking to real families that don't have the ability to save up half of their paycheck and put it in the bank. If they did they wouldn't have problems to start with.

Okay, so we have that first step established—save up an emergency fund. Once you have started saving, if you don't have a debit card consider getting one. A debit card looks and feels just like a credit card and usually has a Visa or MasterCard network name on it. You can use this card for purchases online and for other things. The beauty of a debit card is that you're spending money in your checking account. Once you use the card to buy something, that amount is automatically withdrawn from your account. So be wary; it's not the same as a regular credit card. Debit cards are much more efficient than paying by check and you don't have to carry cash around or make a trip to the bank or ATM as long as you have money in the bank. Speaking of ATMs, you should be careful choosing the machines you withdraw money from—they may attach surcharges to your account. Those surcharges add up. That's just wasting money. Use the machine at your bank or request cash back at the point of a transaction, such as a grocery store, if the merchant allows it.

The most wonderful thing about living without credit cards is simple; you don't have to pay off that debt. Credit card debt has been strangling the financial life out of people for decades. Many people have thousands of dollars charged on their cards and can only make the minimum payment. Charging that much was the first mistake, making the minimum payment is the second big mistake. You have to be prepared to make more than the minimum payment or you'll be paying them off for what feels like forever and most of that money goes to finance charges.

When thinking about life without credit cards I often remember how my grandparent's generation lived. They didn't use credit cards. Heck, credit cards as we know them weren't even invented yet. The only thing they may have owed money on was their house. For example, they bought cars with cash. That idea may seem preposterous considering the price of cars today but it's not impossible. It takes discipline and the ability to say no to the things that you really don't need, which frees you to save money. If you bought a new car you'd probably get a loan for three to five years, maybe more. The longer the loan the less the loan payment, but you end up paying more over the term of the loan. Most people worry about the monthly payment rather than what the cost of the car will be after the loan is paid off. If you get a long-term loan, your budget is strung up for that amount of time. How are you going to feel when you find out that the $15,000 car you bought really cost you $20,000 after finance charges? It's a burden. If you are shopping for a car and you are trying to fit it into your budget by extending the loan, then you simply can't afford that car. Instead, drive the car you have now until the bitter end, and while you are doing that start making substantial monthly payments into your bank account—as if it were a car loan. You should start now rather than later. This strategy will save you money in the long run and keep you out of debt. By the time your car dies, employing this technique may not allow you to be able to buy a brand-new car but you will be able to afford something that fits your needs. I always use the term "drive your car until the wheels fall off." It's a figure of speech, of course. I don't recommend putting you or your family in harm's way with an unsafe vehicle. I can tell you that most cars these days can last 10 years or more, so drive that bulk of steel into the ground. Repair it when needed, and you will be far ahead.

Differentiating Needs from Wants

I've touched on the subject of wants versus needs before, but now I'd like to drill down on it. Most Americans suffer from the "want syndrome." It's debilitating—seriously. Some people get so obsessed with what they want that they lose focus on their needs. They literally start to believe that they need a certain type of vehicle or brand of clothing; they make themselves totally convinced. Unfortunately, the consequences are that they don't have enough money for their basic needs.

It doesn't have to be that way. One of my favorite sayings is "When the money is in your pocket, you're the boss." For the full effect, this slogan needs to always be said in a heavy New York accent to pay respect to the gentleman who first told me these words I live by. For example, my wife and I were at an art festival. I liked a chair that would replace what had been in our living room for a long time. The vendor wanted $360. That seemed excessive to me but the chair was handmade with six materials. The workmanship was unusual and the chair was unique. Now, did I really need a chair that cost $360? Of course I didn't. Nobody does, but as I said it was different. So there I was on a hot summer afternoon, the art festival was winding up, the crowds were starting to leave and the vendor looked hungry for a sale. I also liked a few works of art displayed on the wall of his booth. One piece was $35; another larger one was $100. Did I need the chair? Did I need either of the artworks? No, but I have to admit, I wanted them. Now there I was, getting all the prices for everything I wanted. Note, I specifically said *wanted*. I did not say *needed*. So we started going back and forth on the prices. He wanted $360 for the chair. I said throw in the $35 piece and the chair and I will give you $250 total. He looked at me and said he couldn't do it. He said he can do the chair at $360 and he will throw in the piece. I said no. He then retreated to $320; I said no again. Finally he said, okay I'll do the package deal at $300 for the chair and the smaller piece of art. I said to him, I'll do the deal at $300 if you throw in the bigger piece of artwork rather than the smaller one. He looked at me in a very hard and stern manner and said, "You are tough." I said, "Yes I am." At this point my wife felt compelled to say to him: "You haven't seen anything yet. You have no idea what I have to live with!" We all started laughing and began to make arrangements for delivery the next day.

So what occurred is that I bought a chair that I did not need but wanted and an oversized wonderful piece of artwork that I didn't need and truthfully could have lived without—but could afford! I also let the vendor negotiate against himself to get the price I was comfortable with paying. I initially threw out a low price for the chair. He lowered his price three times. I never countered on any of his price reductions until we got to a price that I felt was reasonable. Then I slammed in another piece of merchandise to finish off the deal in my favor. If I wasn't comfortable or satisfied with the price, I would have never spent the money. Why? I didn't need the merchandise, but they would be very nice additions to my home. In the end I negotiated a price that seemed fair and that I could afford. No damage done financially. I could have easily walked away from the deal if I chose to.

Now let's start taking a look at your basic needs. We are not just talking in a primitive sense; we want to cover the elements that you need to survive day to day. As I said earlier, the chair and the art were not basic needs but I could afford them and still pay for the following:

- Food
- Shelter
- Clothing
- Employment
- Medical
- Transportation
- Communication
- Entertainment

Okay, that's about it—unless you have a special need. It's really not a large list and you could expand or have subheadings under each of those points listed, but we'll break it down as we go along.

The first on the list is food. We obviously need food to survive but you don't need, as I've stated before, to go out to lunch every day of the week. We discussed how to properly shop for food and the variety of ways to save money on food. It's really not difficult you just have to be disciplined and pay attention.

Next on the list is shelter. In the past, millions of Americans got themselves into some nasty predicaments because they bought homes that they couldn't afford. They took out exotic mortgages and decided not to analyze the downside to these mortgages, which were costly and had a negative impact on cash flow. They were so enamored of what they *thought* they could buy (note, I said buy, not afford) that they decided to ignore the fatal risks. Mortgage brokers and others didn't help matters, but those who chose these mortgages should have been wary—remember, if it sounds too good then it probably is. They needed to take some personal responsibility for their actions rather than place all the blame on the commissioned sales person charged with either selling them the dream property or convincing them that they could afford to finance it. In the end, they were the people who agreed to the deal.

You should make certain that the details of a mortgage or other document are transparent and can be deciphered. Take time to understand the transaction. Don't let so-called experts lead you around by your nose—you become the expert; inform yourself so you can avoid such catastrophes. If you are truthful with yourself, you know what you can and can't afford. If you're making a combined $45,000 a year, then a $450,000 house is not realistic even if the bank says it will lend you the money. But many people went for it anyway and the results were foreclosures. Just use common sense when purchasing anything from a home to a lawnmower. Don't get caught up in the "buy your dream home" mentality, because for the most part that's not real. If you notice on advertisements or on TV commercials, the "dream home" always comes with a pool, first rate landscaping, and all the amenities you could want. What's wrong with a quaint home that you can afford—nothing! Keep it simple and you will be happier in the end.

Also, don't forget that you can always rent. There is nothing wrong with renting a house or an apartment. I know of a couple who have rented a small home for 10 years. They couldn't be happier. The landlord is attentive to their needs, the house is close to where they work, and best of all, they can afford it. Another well-off couple I know decided to sell their home after 15 years because they simply got tired of the maintenance. They now live in an apartment and couldn't be happier. Remember, from now on you are living within your means and what you want may not always fit in your budget—that's the reality.

Now let's move on to clothing. You don't need to dress like the people you see on TV or the in-crowd at your job. Being fashionable is a state of mind. If you are confident in yourself and have a healthy dose of self-esteem, you can look like a million bucks regardless of what you are wearing or what you are worth. Dress yourself up from the inside out. You have gone through some unfortunate situations and you're probably hurting inside and that's where you need to start. Of course you can't physically dress yourself up on the inside, but you can start healing. That's what I want to help you do— mend yourself and acquire a new outlook on life, one that doesn't require money to be the sole focus. Once you take that path and become determined to succeed, it will show on the outside. A new pair of shoes or jeans can't fix what's broken on the inside.

I had a young man as a client, and like many of my clients he was mentally and physically distraught over his financial mess. After we talked for a while I noticed that he wore a new pair of fancy shoes. He was sitting with his legs crossed and he kept brushing imaginary dirt off the shoes. It was as if he wanted them to stay perfect. I mentioned the shoes and he said that a person can tell a lot about a man by the type of shoes he wears. I admit that I chuckled. He wanted to know what was funny and if I thought that sentiment was silly or untrue. I told him I thought it was contrived by the media and the people who make shoes. If I went around looking at people's shoes to see what type of person they were, I'd never get a chance to speak with anyone, let alone get to know them. He worried so much about what other people might think about him and his clothes that he forgot about himself. He bought into what he read in fashion magazines or what he saw on a television program. I'd heard that sentiment and read it, but in the real world—not the fashion world or the world of entertainment and glitz where the "in" crowd gathers thinking about, of all things, shoes!— its meaning is empty. Shoes are for comfort. I wear boat shoes, but that doesn't mean I'm an avid boater or daring guy. They are comfortable and slip on and off easily.

Let me hammer the point home again—it's what's on the inside that counts. There are plenty of men and women who look extremely attractive from the outside but once you start to find out what's inside them, well, they aren't so glamorous. I buy clothes that I can afford and that I hope look good on me. I don't look at name brands or tags. When I meet people I look into their eyes and I listen to what they have to say. I think that's a better way to judge a person. I don't look them over to see if they're flaunting the latest fashion. I really don't care about fashion; I care about what a person says and what their actions lead to.

You are reading this book because you want to become more financially savvy; you want independence, and independence breeds confidence. Wearing the most expensive outfit in the world can't match the feeling you will have when you become financially fit and independent.

Voltaire, the magnificent French writer and historian, wrote: "Work banishes those three great evils: boredom, vice, and poverty." If you think about that, you can see the utter reality in it. You may not especially enjoy your job (and we will focus more on this point), but without it you would inevitably be bored, which leads to trouble (vice). For example, if you are not working maybe you'll decide to sit and watch television all day. That may not seem like much of a vice, but where is your productivity; how are you contributing to society? Forget society; how are you contributing to your family and to yourself? That's where the trouble lies; you become valueless and as a consequence you feel that way, too! Your mind, body, spirit, and wallet are in poverty.

If you sit around all day then you are literally watching other people work—the actors on TV are doing their jobs, the lawn maintenance people outside are earning a living, even the postman who delivers your mail; everyone is busy doing something to make money. In order to feel valuable you must do something that equates to value, such as finding employment. If you have a job, that's great; perhaps you can learn new skills, exert yourself more so you can get a raise, or find a new position that offers more money and better benefits. I know that is easier said than done, but you have to be hungry and you have to be willing to outperform the next person. You can volunteer to do different tasks or take on work that is associated with another department; this way you are making yourself more valuable to the company and expanding your knowledge.

If you're not currently working, it's time to search for a job that fits your skill set. Or maybe for a job that doesn't, because right now it's imperative that you find something so you can start earning again. There are arguments against taking a job that's not in line with your past jobs—aspects such as salary requirements come into play and they could be in jeopardy once you get yourself back on track and ready to accept a job that is commensurate with your experience. Well, in desperate times you sometimes have to take desperate measures. If you have to take a $10,000 salary decrease, then you have to suck it up. It's not easy but if that's the reality, so be it. Earning something is better than not earning anything.

More importantly, if you have kids at home you need to provide them with a role model. Is a good role model one who sits around all day and watches television, or is it the person that does what they need to do in order to put food on the table? Remember this saying: Oatmeal is better than no meal.

Many people don't like to work, or they don't like to work at their job because their job is unfulfilling or tedious and joyless. Think about the alternative—not having a job and being bored, probably scared because you don't know how you will pay your bills and, yes, you are in debt. The fact is that you must find employment to pay the bills and to give yourself some degree of freedom to enjoy yourself on a day off. I think most of you understand that and are willing to work hard to get yourself back to some sort of financial significance. It's worth the effort, even if the one blessing is that you can look yourself in the mirror and say, "I'm trying my best." And you can believe it with all your heart.

Before we leave this discussion I want to focus on one of the most controversial and discussed aspects about work: the idea of doing something that you love so it won't seem like work—in other words, the "dream job." People like to discuss their dream job, and that's fine with me but those jobs aren't the norm. Don't get so overwhelmed with searching for that coveted position that you fail to see other jobs that would fill many of your needs and wants. I've heard teachers, police officers, biologists, and even factory workers discuss how their job is like a dream because it covers everything they enjoy doing. I've also heard other people who did those same jobs complain incessantly about them because they never lived up to their expectations. You never know. People are different. So are their expectations of life as well as their needs and wants.

Let me tell you a quick story. I have a friend who opened a tavern. This was his dream—it's his own place and he's the boss and he makes the rules; he even decides what's on the menu. It's nothing fancy but he has high expectations: He wants the food to be memorable and the service to be pleasant and efficient, and he's a clean freak, so the place must be spotless. He's a level-headed guy and understands people fairly well. The tavern has been open for about a year so it seems that it's going smoothly so far. I talk with him occasionally and he said that he's established a local clientele, which is important, and they enjoy the atmosphere and the food.

I decided to go visit after work one Friday. I sat in the corner and watched him working and could immediately tell that he was under a heap of stress. For one thing the bartenders were not functioning well together and he had to help pour drinks, and then I noticed that a new waiter wrote down the wrong order for a table of six—they weren't happy and he couldn't adapt or improvise on his feet. People at the bar were complaining that their food was taking too long. The cooks had done their jobs because the meals were waiting at the pickup station but the bartenders didn't have time to retrieve them fast enough—although one bartender was trying her best. In the meantime the food was getting cold. There were other issues too: broken glass, a customer who wouldn't stop using foul language, and the need for my friend to be in five places at once. This is what he deals with every day. Although it might not always be as busy, my friend is there seven days a week for the lunch and dinner crowd.

I had two drinks and was exhausted from watching him work when I left. I spoke with him about it the next day. He said something which I thought spoke volumes; he said that opening up and running a tavern was his dream but the people that he worked with did not share that dream. The bartenders, wait staff, cooks, and busboys were all there for different reasons and they did not value that place or take their jobs as seriously as he took his job. To them it was just a job. They were mostly young kids just out of high school, struggling to find their way or in college working part-time. He could replace them but then he'd just end up hiring more of the same. They weren't bad; they just didn't have the passion. He was still fine-tuning them, and he was also coming to the realization that his dream is a tenuous one and that he needs other people to make it come true. That was difficult for him to admit, but it doesn't prevent him from trying. Unfortunately, the fact is that the food industry is riddled with transient workers. Very few people grow up thinking that they want to be a dishwasher. They just end up there and leave when a new opportunity presents itself.

Dream jobs are hard to come by, and every job is going to have its peaks and valleys. You may love your job but hate your boss. Don't get caught up in the dream; there's a good chance you will have to scratch and claw before you get anywhere near a dream job. But that's what we're doing; we're fighting to get back on top, back in control. Remember this: The next time you volunteer to do more or try to get ahead at your job and are ridiculed because your fellow workers think you're kissing up to the boss, forget them. They may not value the job like you do or need the income like you do. They are happy in mediocrity, and in mediocrity they'll stay. That night in the tavern I noticed one bartender doing twice as much work as the other (I mentioned earlier that one bartender was making a valiant effort to retrieve the food). I revealed that to my friend and he said the hustling bartender was recently divorced and raising two kids on her own. She needed the job and worked like her very life depended on it. Do you think she aspired as a young girl to become a bartender? I doubt it, but there's nothing wrong with the hospitality and restaurant business. As for the other bartender, well, she's looking for a new job. It pays in different ways when you take your job seriously.

Another serious aspect of working is receiving medical insurance. That's certainly a benefit and one that you, and your family, may come to rely upon. If your employer doesn't offer medical insurance, then you'll have to investigate other options. Call insurance providers and inquire about pricing and their various coverage packages.

If you are unemployed, ask about government assistance or other aid you may be eligible to receive. You can go to the library and use the computer (or use your own) to find information on medical insurance and financial assistance, discounted or free medication programs, and health-plan information. Some communities have health-care clinics that serve those who need treatment but don't have insurance. I don't recommend not having medical insurance, as one hospital visit can cost you thousands of dollars. Take advantage of what's available until you find employment that offers medical.

Now let's move to the ever-controversial transportation topic. I think you know where I stand on the SUV subject. I'm still baffled by how many families bought into the "I need a mini-monster truck to cart my two kids around." Maybe it was the advertising, the sense of empowerment because of their sheer size, or the leasing deals. Regardless, let's get one thing straight—purchasing a new car is a losing deal. As soon as you drive off the lot the car's value plummets. It's a fact. If you lease a car then you have strict guidelines to adhere to or you will get crushed by all sorts of fees. I'm not going to get into a shouting match with anyone regarding buying new, used, or leasing—it's like arguing about religion or politics; everyone has a strong opinion and they will rarely change their minds even when the facts are placed in front of them. You can go online and investigate the pros and cons of buying new and used or leasing. The point I want to make is that overextending yourself because you want a slick sports car or trendy four-by-four leads only to financial calamity.

You can make a list of the wants and needs for your next car. For example, a top-of-the-line stereo system may be a want, but you may need an economical yet reasonably powerful engine. The pros of getting such an engine are better fuel economy and the confidence that it will last without major maintenance requirements. The stereo system could set you back another $500 to $1,000—money you could be saving. The bottom line is deciding what's more important. It's obvious. This may sound like first-grade stuff that's easy to figure out, but the fact is when people get to a dealership and start looking at cars they get giddy. We've all experienced that feeling—you look at the latest models and think wow, I'd look cool in that! Sure you would; that's why they produce such vehicles. Start *thinking* with a clear head. You are being seduced and the car salespeople are the facilitator of that fantasy. They'll do whatever it takes to seat you in that car or truck, even spread out loan payments up to seven years and not require a large down payment. By the time the seven years are done and if you still own the car, you will have paid nearly double what the sticker price was, when you consider the interest rate and all the other changes you get talked in to paying for. Also let's not forget about insurance. Insurance can be like walking on a landmine unless you call your insurance company before you buy a new vehicle and get a quote. Most people just buy a vehicle without realizing that their insurance is going to increase. Combine the payment for the vehicle and the cost of the insurance and you may be in for a big surprise. You don't realize what you got yourself into until it's too late.

A long-term loan is not the answer. Nearly 40 percent of the people who own cars are in an "upside-down loan." This means that you owe more on the car than it's worth. Remember when I said the value of a new car takes a nosedive as soon as you drive it off the lot? Well, I bought a used car, and the short story is that the car had been sold two months earlier to a good customer of the salesman. That owner traded it in for a larger car, and the car I bought had only 900 miles. The dealership dropped 30 percent off the original price, so I bought a great car that was two months old with 900 miles at a nice discount. Depreciation continues over the years, and if you try to trade that car in before the end of the loan you'll probably owe more than it's worth. You'll be stuck with that car or truck even if you can't afford to maintain it. Be smart; I want you to be tough and savvy when it comes to buying a vehicle. If you don't like the deal, walk out of the dealership. You have to be able to say "no." Once you sign the papers no one other than the bank cares if you can make the payments; it's all on you. If you learn one thing from this, remember that you are in control of your money. Don't let anyone tell you that you can afford something or that you will be financially safe with the deal they are proposing. You're the boss. In fact, remember I said earlier, "When money is in your pocket, you're the boss!" The salesperson or finance manager doesn't care about you. You are simply just another commission to them. I don't care if it's a car, a house, or a refrigerator. You make the decision by being informed and fully aware of your budget constraints. Don't make rash decisions on large purchases. Take time to evaluate and run the numbers to make certain you can afford the purchase.

Communication is next on the list. This covers e-mail, phones, and other devices you use to keep in touch with the people you work with, your friends, and your family. I don't think it's possible to sit through a TV show without seeing a commercial for some network offering you the world. First, allow me to say this: Get a grip. You don't need to constantly text or call your friends and family. This whole "keep in touch" thing is as egregious as the selling of bottled water caper. It may be hard for some of you reading this book to believe, but not too long ago cell phones were scarce and texting was nonexistent. I understand that for most business people a cell phone is mandatory. That's fine. But the cell phone and texting abuse that goes on is ridiculous. Remember, people, it's not free. You need to be frugal. If your friends or family can't get over the fact that you won't be texting them 20 times a day or calling a dozen times a week, that's their problem. It's time to cut back and sign up for the bare minimum. We have "Communication" in the need column because it's important, but you have to do your homework and find a network that offers something you can afford. Do you really need the power to text or call someone in Thailand? In fact, most of us don't need international calling. If you do, do it through an inexpensive Internet service and save some money. The abuse of this power has started at an early age, too. I'm sure you've read about teenagers texting one another hundreds of times a week. Do they think about the consequences, the money it's going to cost? Obviously not.

People have told me that it's just the way things are now; people are required to be in constant contact and everyone in your family should have a cell phone "just in case." Ah yes, that "just in case" phrase. You never know what might happen. You might actually forget the broccoli for tonight's dinner and without your cell phone who will you contact to get the broccoli! Dinner will be ruined! Cell phones are great for emergencies, but there were emergencies 20 years ago and most of us didn't have one. I'm not certain broccoli can be considered an emergency, but who knows?

Advertising is feeding you all this information, tapping into your fears and deep emotions, especially when it comes to our kids having cell phones. I've seen six-year-old kids with cell phones and the parents are paying the fees, and then they wonder where their money goes. Let's be honest about this issue. Kids and teenagers who use cell phones are texting jokes, sending answers to questions on tests, gossiping, e-mailing, playing games, taking pictures, or recording fights, and sometimes using them for immoral or illegal activities; it's out of control. For the most part the constant-contact routine is nonsense. Don't buy into it. A cell phone is still a luxury unless you need it for business.

You can still be a part of the human race and be a good parent if you rarely use your cell phone, if all your kids don't have cell phones, and if you don't find it necessary to text a friend what you ate for lunch. I highly doubt that your child in 30 years will say you were a terrible parent as a result of your unwillingness to pay for cell phone services. Better yet, use your children's desire for the device as a learning opportunity. If they want a phone, let them pay for some or all of the equipment and monthly service fees with a part-time job.

One thing to note: I see a trend in having cell phones replace home phone service. Actually, this trend makes sense to me. If you have financial difficulties, why not reduce the expense. In some cases, basic cell phone service is cheaper than land-line service.

I understand that the gadgets you can hold in your hand are amazing—the whole world in your palm is a great advertising campaign. Besides the cost of these things there's another price being paid, and it too is costly. I went to an associate's house and I noticed that a few of the kids there spent the whole time on their cell phones—not as a group but in separate areas of the house. It was a cookout and there were other kids hanging out but they were too busy to communicate with them. They were more interested in what the phones offered them than what human companionship at a cookout offered. The other kids were having a blast getting to know one another and playing in the pool. I thought that it was sad to be more interested in an electronic device than other kids your own age. I mentioned this to someone and they told me it happens all the time. Kids in church, in school, anywhere really, just staring at that thing in the palm of their hand, oblivious to the world around them—that's a good thing?

I received a holiday card one year. It was a picture of a family standing and sitting in their home and everyone held a phone, talking or texting. Although it was a joke, an underlying message is being sent. Is this a reflection of things to come? A family can't take the time to put their phones down to take a family photo? Sad. What's worse are adults chatting away on their cell phones in an office or some other place where it's clearly posted that all cell phones must be turned off. What kind of message are we sending our kids—a text message?

It's great to have something that can give you information on the spot, that immediate satisfaction, but the real world is right in front of you. Some people don't notice that when they're driving their car and simultaneously fooling with their cell phone or other device. You can guess the results. Don't stray off your chosen path. Communication is wonderful, but our society has a bad habit of ratcheting every product up to unnecessary levels, and then "communicating" through advertising that if you're not at that highest level you're missing out on something. Let me communicate a message to you— you're only missing out on the cost.

Last but not least on my list is entertainment. I wanted to add this to the list because you do need to have fun, but like we discussed earlier in the book, fun doesn't always have to cost money. Here's a nice idea I learned from a couple who were financially strapped. When going over their budget, they slashed all restaurant and movie activity—no takeout either. Instead of going to a place filled with people, they invited the people to their home. The wife created easy invitations and dropped them off in the mailboxes of the neighbors who they talked to from time to time. The party plan was simple: Bring a dish, something you like to drink, and a game you enjoy playing. After everyone arrived they would partake in a few drinks and then vote on the game that they would all play after eating from the buffet.

At the first party only three couples arrived, but they had fun. There was plenty of food and drink and they decided to play charades. It was awkward at first because they weren't great friends, more like acquaintances, but by the end of the night the room was filled with laughter. The word spread and more couples and some single people showed up. The parties began to move from one house to another, so everyone took on the burden of setting up for the party and cleaning up. At one of the parties a few of the guys started talking and they expressed thanks to the husband of the original party. These guys revealed that they too were trying to cut back and save money and they felt like a lot of the fun was being cut from their free time. They all agreed that this was a fabulous way to enjoy good company, get a bit goofy, let your guard down, and still save money. I have some family members who are in their fifties now. When the husband first left his place of employment and started his own company, they had two small children and no money coming in. For entertainment, they checked out free videotapes from the library as their weekend activity. Now things have changed. The business is very successful and money has been rolling in. The kids are grown, but they still go to the library, although now they check out DVDs instead of videos.

You see, it doesn't take a lot of cash to drum up good times and great memories. If you don't have friendly neighbors, then maybe you can do something with your family: invest in a few puzzles and stay at home and do "puzzle night" or "board game night." This may sound boring to some of you, but spending quality time with your family and maybe some friends is part of the values we discussed. It's what counts. It's these times the kids will fondly remember, and so will you.

Despite what you see, hear, and read, you really don't need to be entertained. I know, you work hard all week and you want to be treated to something special; you want to be amused or waited on. Every radio station in this country lives by the same mantra—"working for the weekend!" It's Friday night and it's time to go out and let loose. I remember when I was in my twenties, my friends and I would go out from Wednesday to Saturday night and by Sunday our money was gone.

You know what? We didn't have a thing to show for it, except maybe a headache and circles under our eyes from a lack of sleep. Certainly not any long-lasting memories remained, for obvious reasons I would rather avoid discussing in these pages!

To avoid the feeling of emptiness, try to get something in return when you contemplate your entertainment options. My clients' return was a closer relationship with their neighbors, a sense of amusement that they hadn't experienced in a long while, and the feeling of gratification through the creation of something that so many people enjoyed and participated in. I don't want it to sound like you can't spend any money on entertainment, but you must be true to your budget. If there are very little resources left over, then you'll have to make do. It's certainly not impossible—go to the beach or a park and make a picnic lunch, and if you crave more excitement look in the newspaper or online for free activities such as music festivals or other events that stimulate your interests. There's plenty to do, so don't mope around on the couch or pace your kitchen floor—get out and get your mind and body active. It's part of the process and it will strengthen you; it will make you more independent and less reliant on the norm or what is typically offered for a price. Remember your hobby ideas; they could be your new source of entertainment. Speaking of free activities: The relatives I mentioned earlier informed me that in their town the movie theater allows those 50 years of age or older free screenings of first-run movies on Tuesdays. Guess what they do each and every Tuesday?

Okay, we went over our needs. You may be able to fiddle with the needs list a bit, but when it comes down to the things that are necessary to survive, there's not a whole lot of leeway. But that's not the case with the "wants" in life. Here's where things get out of control—and you are also outnumbered. It's you the consumer against every advertising powerhouse in the world, broadcasting their promises of a better life and a more rewarding and satisfying life *if* you buy their products. I mean, how can you possibly live without the latest and greatest gadget that chops, dices, and slices your vegetables, cheeses, bread, fruits, and nuts? This gadget makes eating healthy so much easier and it's a snap to clean. And with that gadget you'll get two more gadgets that will make your life a dream—all for $19.95. In three months all those gadgets will either be broken or thrown into one of your cabinets.

The bottom line is that spending makes some people feel satisfied. It makes them believe, for a moment, that they have the power to buy what they *want* without worry or without repercussions. Having money in a certain way is an escape from the real world. Not having money, unfortunately, has the opposite effect. This spending power purifies their spirit and annihilates all worry about debt or bills—if they can buy these shoes and this purse or this weightlifting machine or surround-sound system then they must not be in debt or have financial problems. It's only after the purchase, when the flush and passion of buying have subsided, that they realize what a huge mistake they just made. Then the guilt sets in and the anxiety starts to rise from their chest.

Some people don't even buy the things that they want because of the joy they will get from them. They simply buy because they have a perceived notion that they deserve to buy things; it's their right as a consumer. That notion has been drilled into our thought process and is activated as soon as we walk into a showroom or a store. You've seen it on television and heard it on the radio since you were a child. You deserve these *things*—whatever they may be, a new watch or television or dishwasher. You work hard, you deserve such products. Hell, you deserve the best! Don't settle for second best. Why buy something that's not up to your standards just because you can afford it? Go for the things you can't afford. Only the best of us deserve the top of the line, the finest that money can buy. We all like to think of ourselves as deserving, as the best, right? You don't think of yourself as a loser or someone who deserves that rinky-dink product in the corner, the one that is "so out of style." Multi-million-dollar advertising campaigns have been pushing those buttons for years. They've been brainwashing you with their slogans: You're worth it; When only the best will do; Tell her that you love her with a diamond; For the sophisticated shopper.

Let me tell you, it's a load of garbage! Sure, some of the new products are amazing and, if you buy the right ones, they could save you money over a long period of time and probably improve your quality of life. But you have to be able to afford them when you do in fact buy them. Don't let commercials or ads make decisions for you. It's okay to want things but you have to draw the line. You can fill your house or your apartment with all the things that you want and still be the most miserable person in town. Once the bills start pouring in, all the bliss is drained.

Here's another tip about buying the things that you want. Let's say you are walking around the mall thinking about buying a pair of shoes or an outfit—men's or women's. You come to a store that you like and notice that it is running a mammoth sale. Oh happy day, it's a sale. My advice is to run the other way unless you have the willpower of a monk. Here's the reason: When stores run such sales, you end up spending much more than if there was no sale at all—especially if you are contained in one store. They've got you where they want you and you probably won't leave unless someone drags you out of there.

A store runs a huge sale to get customers in the door. Once customers are in the door, the salespeople keep on lining up the products. You bought an outfit on sale; well, guess what, they have the perfect shoes to go with that outfit. You probably don't want to buy only one outfit because the prices are so low they may never be that low again! Then there are jackets and scarves and gloves, jewelry, and check out that sweater—he'll look fabulous in that sweater. You are overcome and you are saving money, tons of money, right?

Wrong. Chances are you just spent two or three months' worth of your budget on clothing and still didn't get the things you really need for work or for kicking around the house. You bought things that look really great, especially for going out, which costs money, too. You may be able to wear some of the stuff to work but as you were shopping, work wasn't on your mind. You didn't have a plan because once you saw those sale signs and all that colorful merchandise you suffered a brain drain. You were on overload. What started out as a shopping session for shoes turned into much more. You could have walked out of the mall with a pair of $70 shoes but you ended up walking out with over $300 worth of on-sale merchandise that you probably didn't need.

Be prepared for those moments. Sales aren't always a good thing unless it's for something that you "need." If you come across a "want" that is on sale and you have been saving your money and can cover the cost, make the purchase—good for you. Otherwise steer clear and use your better judgment. Sometimes abstinence is the better path. If you don't need or really don't want, stay out of stores. It's just like when you walk into the supermarket and are confronted with sale items. Before you know it you spend much more than you wanted to because the sale items were too good to pass up. The only problem is that they probably weren't on your list. It's a trap that I don't want you to fall for. If you're at the supermarket stick to your list; if you're going to the mall make a list. Go into the store and buy what you need and then leave. Be strong and be smart.

Chapter FIVE

Teach Your Children Well

Y ou are probably not on this road alone; chances are you have children (young or older, it doesn't matter) and perhaps a spouse. If so, then pay special attention. Even if you don't have children, it's a good idea to focus on this chapter because they may be in your future.

Children are born inquisitive: They watch, touch, feel, taste, and have a shrewd perception of what's going on around them. I'm not a child psychiatrist, but I'm telling you that kids know when something's going wrong or out of whack within the family unit. They may confront you about it or they may just hide this nagging feeling inside. It's up to you as the parent to make most family matters as transparent as possible—especially when it comes to finances. Kids listen and they see things. They observe changes and overhear conversations on the phone or in person.

You can't fool a kid. They see other parents driving fancy cars and hear their friends discussing the things their parents bought. It's not unusual for a child to come home and ask his or her parents why they don't have a swimming pool or a new car. When they come home with such questions don't dismiss them with a trite answer; sit them down and explain to them what's going on. Teach your children the value of money and allow them to make this journey with you. It will most certainly prepare them and shed light on what's really important in life. Remember, there are things more valuable than money. Life lessons are certainly one of those things. Life lessons learned early on during the impressionable years can be extremely valuable once they become adults. Don't deprive a child of this opportunity to learn.

Talk to Your Kids about Money

A client of ours used to lock herself in her room for hours with all of her bills and agonize over the fact that she couldn't pay them. She would spread them over her bed and think of ways to make ends meet but the ends just wouldn't come together. She cried a lot because of the helpless feeling that would drape over her. She discussed this with one of our counselors and then admitted that her five-year old-son used to knock on the door and ask what was wrong. She wouldn't admit to him what was bothering her and usually told him to go watch television or busy himself with his toys.

That response seemed natural at first. She's protecting her son from the unforgiving realities of life. Why afflict a five-year-old with an adult's troubles? Fair enough, but if you think that five-year-old is just going to dismiss his mother's incessant crying behind a locked bedroom door then you had better think again. A great amount of psychological damage can occur when a child hears his mother sobbing night after night. What kind of impression will that leave? Think about the message being sent— crying behind a locked door is the proper way to resolve financial challenges, or all challenges, for that matter.

After her bout of crying, the client always tried to sneak out of her room without speaking to the boy, thinking that everything was over until the next time she started crying. But that wasn't the case, and she soon learned the hard way when this bomb was dropped on her: One day she received a phone call from school; it was her child's teacher. The teacher said that she saw the boy off by himself at recess and went over to ask him if everything was okay. When she approached the boy she noticed he was softly crying. When the teacher asked what was wrong, the boy replied that he was crying because his mother was in trouble. Most children believe their parents are invincible. They believe they have the answer to any question and that nothing can hurt them. All of a sudden that belief, which has been reinforced over and over, is being questioned.

This, of course, nearly tore the heart out of our client. She was devastated and asked our counselor what she could do to help dissipate the boy's pain. Our counselor asked if she ever discussed her financial problems with her child. She said no because she thought he was too young to understand and why bother the boy with *her* problems and pressures. You notice the bolding and the italics on the word *her*? I did that on purpose because the problems were not just hers, but her son's as well, because he lived with his mother and witnessed her suffering. The boy may not have been able to fully understand the depths of her money problems, but from his perspective, he couldn't imagine what horrible things were making his mother cry.

To a kid's imagination, money is low on the totem pole when it comes to those dark and mysterious things that make people so frightened they weep. Money is nothing compared to what hides beneath the bed or in the closet. Money is real, and it's not scary to a kid. Think of it from a kid's point of view—quarters and pennies and so on don't terrorize kids, and if they did they would just chuck them down the road and that would be the end of it.

By hiding her mundane crisis, she actually contributed to the spawning of the terrible scenarios that her child started playing out in his mind. Something awful was torturing his mother and in a sense the boy was right, but it wasn't a six-legged beast with huge, ghastly blood-shot eyes—it was scarier, the Debt Monster.

After she realized her mistake our client sat down with her son and talked about their money situation. The boy understood and also decided to help his mom save money by not begging her to buy him candy or ice cream. He realized that he didn't need a new bike; the bike he had was good enough. They made a pact together swearing that they'd do their best to save money by turning off the lights, not leaving the television on, and other things. The boy became a part of the solution; he was no longer worried for his mother and, as a matter of fact, his mother stopped closing the door and weeping over her bills. She spread them out on the kitchen table and started to analyze how she could slowly get herself out of debt. She also began the arduous process of building a budget and included her son on it. They did it together.

Kids are smart; they can perceive even the most subtle changes in the household. They may not speak up about it for fear of being out of line or for their own personal reasons, but they know. Parents often discuss things behind closed doors but kids can hear; the walls and the doors aren't that thick, especially when the parents raise their voices. So if you alter your spending habits—no more Friday pizza or renting movies—it sends a message to your kids that something could be wrong. Be a strong parent. Don't hide it from them or ignore their questions or shy, tentative inquiries. If they want to talk, make time to talk. Provide them with more than a quick five minutes; that won't suffice. You have to sit down with them and explain what is happening in terms they can fully understand in order to comfort them.

When I was younger, my family ran into tough times after my father died. In a two-year period my remaining family went from an upper-middle-class family without a financial care to a family that could have qualified for welfare. I remember the heat being turned off in the middle of February because the bill wasn't paid. My mother played it off as an oversight, but it was apparent to me what was happening. We never spoke of that very chilly month after the heat was turned back on, but it certainly left an impression. I think that experience taught me valuable lessons and may be the reason I began financial counseling, which I've been doing for more than 25 years. It's interesting how a few instances in a child's life can mold and shape them as adults. I enjoy helping others. I don't want to see you or anyone else get caught in these types of situations.

By choosing not to include your children in conversations, you leave them with no other option than to create their own reasons why you are cutting back on spending—maybe mom or dad lost their job, maybe the family is going to be kicked out of their house or apartment, and the list goes on and the anxiety grows. In my situation, my mother didn't discuss it with us and we were left to guess. Looking back now, from my professional perspective, that wasn't the right thing to do, but that was another generation. That's why I'm imparting this lesson to you. Kids can take a lot, they are a tough bunch. They have an uncanny ability to bounce back, but they usually are not prepared to cope with the burden of secrecy. If you are upfront and honest, that provides them with something tangible to think about. They can then start the wheels turning to help solve the crisis instead of wondering about what is going on.

When you sit down with your kids to discuss your money situation, be honest, but don't be all doom and gloom. Show them what you are up against and how you have started to deal with the financial issues and unstable times. If you have a strategy, share it with them and also include the things that will impact them—such as cutting back on buying junk food or how things will change during the holidays. Don't be afraid; take control of the situation, because if you're not in control, if you are not leading the way, then the kids will wonder who is in charge. Tell them that the family will succeed; it may be uncomfortable but the family will rise above this unfortunate situation and be stronger than ever. Do your best to try to make them part of the solution. This is a great way to take a bad situation that's affecting the family and turn it into a positive outlook and a determination to succeed.

You can also ease your child's fears by letting them know that your family is not alone in this battle. Millions of other families, maybe even some of their friends' families, are going through this same drama. It's also an appropriate time to let them know that hardships happen, even if you had a prosperous career and that preparing for financial hardships is smart. They have to understand that the cliché that "money does not grow on trees" is true. But of course you also want to tell them that this is a private matter. It's certainly nothing to be embarrassed about, but explain to them that this stays within the family; this is your own private battle, something that is only to be shared among family members.

I can't stress this enough: Stay positive. If you stay poised and maintain the leadership position, then your children will notice and it will make them feel better and more confident. Try not to argue with your spouse—I'm not a marriage counselor, but I am positive that the anxiety and fear that emanates throughout the home because of fighting is detrimental to your cause. Remain optimistic even when things look bleak, especially when matters that you don't have much power over, such as the economy and the rising cost of gas and groceries, are not helping your cause. Because you can inspire your children by show-ing them that no matter how tough it gets, you will keep working hard and looking on the bright side. They will remember that and appreciate it when they are parents. They may even have a few good stories to tell about the journey you took together.

Kids and Values

This is a nice segue into teaching your children values. Just as adults are overrun by television ads, advertising, and day-to-day promotions on the newest and coolest cars, shoes, makeup, and garden tools, kids deal with the same things. They see new bicycles, dolls, race cars, video games, and phones. They see it on television and sometimes they see it in person when one of their friends presents a new gadget that your family can't afford. It can be unsettling, and it may make the kids a bit angry and jealous. When you start seeing those emotions surface, it's time to sit your kids down and have a little talk. It may be a good idea to talk with them before those emotions manifest themselves.

It's not easy for a kid to understand why some peo-ple have more money than others; it doesn't seem fair. You, as a parent, have to explain the details on why the things that money can buy aren't everything in life. We went over this earlier in the book: The value in life lies in your family, friends, and the things that you hold dear. If you give your kids love and attention, that will more than make up for the video games the neighbor's kids are playing. Forget the video games; go to the park and toss a Frisbee around. That's spending time with your kids. They will remember that long after the video game is outdated or broken. Those are the memories that are cherished.

Try increasing your child's knowledge about the value of money. I was recently speaking with a friend who informed me that his daughter wanted a new computer. He wanted to get her a Dell for about $500. She wanted an Apple computer at a cost of $1,200. Apparently, there is a certain cachet or coolness with owning an Apple computer in your teens. It wears off quickly when the teenager has to buy it for themselves. I suggested that he let her buy the Apple after she saves up the difference in price. When that happens, my friend will then contribute the $500 he was going to spend toward the Dell. The daughter will learn firsthand about the value of saving, the cost of fulfilling desires, and hopefully how hard it is to part with hard-earned cash.

If you spend time with them and share with them, they won't care as much about the ancillary products being promoted on television, and those jealous and angry feelings will dissipate. These are valuable years, and it's up to you to instill in them the true value of life—not what the television ads profess to be of value. It's not easy, especially if you are competing with other parents who have more, but as an adult you have to question what they have more of. If you are intimidated or a bit jealous of the materialistic things that other families have, you need to give yourself a reality check. If you are giving your children all the love and time you can spare, you are providing them with the most important elements in life. You have no need to be jealous or anxious over the fact that you can't provide the material components that advertisers say make children happy. That's crazy.

You are raising your kids to understand the true value of life. You learned your lessons; you possibly made some mistakes and perhaps you coveted items that were simply out of your financial realm, and yet you still purchased them. Did they really bring you joy? Impart to your kids the true nature of life; it's not the purchasing or the receiving—it's the gift of giving love, time, laughter, and joy. Life is precious. To some, life is short. Enjoy it while you are here, but don't forget to instill values unto the next generation.

When speaking with your children about values, you can also start to educate them on the financial aspects of life. There is value in money but it's altogether different from the most essential and important values in life. Kids should learn early that money is significant and the value of having money is more vital than spending money. Teach them about saving and what can happen if they spend without a thought to the consequences. If your children get an allowance, use that as an example. If they spend their allowance in one day, they are out of money until they earn their allowance again. Teach them to be thrifty and smart with their money. Just don't give them the allowance; make them earn it. They will appreciate the fact that they are actually doing something to earn their allowance. If they fail to do their chores, don't pay them. When you go food shopping, show them how you are saving money by choosing one brand over another or by purchasing the item that's on sale. When your child picks out something he or she wants, take the time to explain to them that it's not on your shopping list. You have a plan and you want to stick with it. Show discipline; it will rub off on your children and teach them lessons that they will use throughout their adulthood.

Prepare Your Teenagers

Teenagers are a different story when compared to younger children. They are in the line of fire. Credit card companies have been pursuing teenagers and designing credit cards so they can "learn" about the credit system, and although most teenagers don't fully understand the repercussions of using a credit card and the impact it can have on their future financial situations, more teens are working and are spending their own money. Credit card companies believe that they have hit the jackpot.

It's likely that your high school junior or senior has been offered a cosigned card solicited through the Internet and mailings addressed to you, the parents. Because of this new trend of marketing to teens, one of out of three high school seniors use credit cards, and half of them have cards in their own names. That, to me, is trouble for the teen and potentially for the parents because they—and that means you—could be legally responsible for the account.

For the record, I am not a fan of handing out credit cards to children, regardless of their age. Children should be taught the lesson of saving, not spending. It is clear to me, though, that paper currency is going to become a tool of the past, and we will for the most part become a cashless society. Teaching our younger generation about the use of a financial vehicle that looks like it will be paving the way for the future can only be helpful. You just have to proceed with caution. Credit card use in the hands of the inexperienced can be hazardous, regardless of whether it's an adult or a child.

Here are a few things that you can do to help prepare your teen if and when you decide to move in this direction—and let me caution you, take care of your own financial situation first. I want to add this section because the day will come when you will be monetarily sound again and may have to make such decisions.

- First, make certain that the teen has a checking account. Teens should first understand the basic skills of writing a check and tracking money in a bank account and using such skills as a type of "financial training wheel."
- After they have demonstrated the ability to balance a checkbook, let them use a debit card, which looks and acts like a credit card but is tied to the checking account. Teach them how to reconcile their bank account. If you don't know how, ask your branch manager for help.

- When the teen has mastered those basics, apply for an extra credit card under your name (the parent's) on an account at a store or bank. Make certain that the credit card has a low spending limit to avoid getting yourself into trouble and hurting your credit rating.
- Tell the teen the basics of how the card works—starting with the connection between charging one month and paying the next. Emphasize that it's not free money unless the balance is paid in full before the grace period expires. Explain interest and how it adds up if the debt continues to grow. Look at the fine print and review key terms such as late fees.
- Set some ground rules. Is the card reserved for emergencies or specific purposes such as clothes shopping? Emphasize the importance of making certain the card is kept in a safe place. If the credit card is lost or stolen, the first thing you should do is report your missing credit card to the card issuer as soon as you notice the card is missing. Don't wait a day or even a minute. Most card issuers print their customer service phone number on your billing statement. Locate a recent copy of your statement to find the number to reach your card issuer. Alternatively, if you have online access for your credit card, you may be able to use the website to report your missing credit card. When you contact your creditor, you should have the following:
  - Your account number
  - The date you noticed your card was missing
  - The date and amount of your last purchase, if known

Even after you've contacted the card issuer by phone, it's wise to follow up with a letter. The letter should state that your credit card was lost or stolen and include the account number, date of loss or theft, first date the loss was reported, and the last authorized transaction. This letter will provide proof that you reported the loss should that fact ever come into question.

- Set limits and supervise the teen's usage. Monitor what happens when you give them an amount to spend, say $150 on clothes. Do they surpass the limit? If so, you should be prepared to penalize the teen in some manner. This is very important. Young adults must learn early on that the downside of credit cards can be painful. Help develop and advance their level of responsibility.

- When you feel the teen is ready for a card in their name, encourage them to shop around for low rates and fees. Personally, I wouldn't do this until the teen turns 18 and has a job.

- Parents and teens should keep a close eye on limit increases by the credit card company. Just because the card has, for example, a $1,000 limit does not mean that it should be spent. With a limit that high, it could easily be increased to $2,000 or $3,000 within six months, so be careful not to allow this to happen. Think of the damage that could occur.

- Keep in mind that teens may apply for a card in their own name when they turn 18. Don't be surprised to see credit card offers addressed to a son or daughter, well before their 18th birthday. You should keep an eye out for such offers through the mail.

- With credit cards, parents must define what an acceptable purchase is. Pizza at midnight is not a proper purchase. A few years ago, fast-food restaurants did not take credit cards, and now it's hard to find one that does not. This could be a quick way to get into debt.

- You should always be wary and keep a close eye on what your teen is buying over the Internet. You and your teenager could form a pact, meaning that anything bought on the Internet would be revealed. The Internet does have a sinister side and many teens, armed with a credit card, could be sucked into something over their heads and you could be held responsible if you cosigned the card.

- You should also remember that credit card companies who are reaching out to teens or minors with major credit cards must follow the same federal disclosure laws they do for marketing to adults. Whether they are selling by mail, telephone, or the Internet, banks are required to reveal costs such as annual fees and finance charges.

- Emphasize over and over again the importance of a good credit history and how a poor one can ruin their efforts to buy their first car or rent an apartment. Show them how to get a copy of their credit report. Help them figure out how to read the report. If you are not fluent in deciphering the document, go online and review the credit report instructions.

- Give the teen responsibility for paying all or part of their balance from an allowance or job. If the teens aren't earning the money, it's not a beneficial exercise. Most teens don't really appreciate the value of money until they are out working hard and being rewarded with a paycheck. You may have the chance to increase their overall sensitivity to finances early on.

- Overall, use this time and sequence of events as one of your last opportunities to teach your child as they will soon be entering adulthood. Of course, once they enter adulthood, they'll know everything—or so they think. Also, this is a great time to refresh and possibly expand your financial skills when it comes to using these cards of disaster.

Some parents may wonder why I'm making all this fuss over teens and spending. I think you know by now, especially after reading this book, this is not the same world that you and I grew up in. The primary advertising message today is: Buy now! And who cares whether you have enough money, it's not our problem, and it won't be yours for 30 days until the charge card bill hits your mailbox.

Spending is portrayed as an entitlement of young people. The consequences of overspending are not found in the advertising message. Immediate gratification is the only thing that matters. To make that easier, credit card companies single out teens and newly graduated students with their message—Buy now! They don't show the consequences in any of their TV commercials or mailers. I'm not saying they should. It's not their responsibility to teach our young. It is our responsibility as experienced consumers to pass along our knowledge to the younger generation and hope that they will avoid the same traps that ensnared us.

If a teen wants an expensive toy, you should teach your teens to save the money they make from chores or other jobs. When they have the money, the teens can use a credit card or, even better, pay cash. If you are teaching your teen about credit cards, make certain that when the bill comes due, the entire balance is paid off in one shot. This is a good way to postpone the immediate gratification factor. It's okay to want material things but sometimes you just have to wait. If you choose not to wait, within 30 days you must pay for the item in full. That's going to leave a lasting impression.

So, you see, you can bring your younger kids and teens in on this process. It could be very satisfying to instruct them on the finer points of money so they won't suffer the same unfortunate outcomes that you may have suffered through. By teaching your kids about financial responsibility, you will also be giving yourself a review on money matters. Money and financial accountability is a lifelong process. You learn something new all the time because the money industry is always evolving and you need to evolve with it or you will get lost in the mayhem—that's where the trouble begins. By educating your kids, you get the added bonus of preparing them for life lessons that sincerely matter.

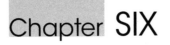

Chapter SIX

Introduction to Banking

Use this section as a guide to help your kids choose the right type of bank to save their money in, and as a learning tool or refresher course for yourself. Some of the topics may not seem relevant now because of your situation, but I think it's important to examine this information for future purposes. You may not be in debt or you will not always be in debt, so I'd like to emphasize some types of loans and options you have to invest your money in once you start getting back on your feet.

You have a number of ways to save your money, invest your money, and keep your money safe. Now that you have seen the worst of what can happen to your finances, it's wise to investigate the avenues available to you and your kids as you start the process of becoming financially fit again.

The optimal benefit that you can get from this section is a general education on the banking system and a means to begin building a suitable knowledge-base for your children. Remember, the more that you are informed the better off you are, because in the world of money and finances you are usually on your own to make good choices and bad choices. The more wisdom you have, the better choices you will make. Believe me, I have seen it all and I want you to become smarter and pass that intelligence down to your kids.

First let me start with an example. At a recent gathering with some friends I met a couple who recognized me from the advertising we do. They started talking about saving money in the bank and about their retirement accounts. They confided how surprised they were at how much money they lost in their two IRA accounts. I asked them if they were familiar with what stocks or bonds they were investing in, and they said "no." They just let the financial manager of the company take care of that for them. I then asked them if they check their IRA accounts often to see how they are doing, and again they answered "no." They just figured they would be doing fine.

Okay, that's an example of what I don't want you to do. Don't just put money into a bank account or IRA and hope it will grow. You have to have a handle on your money. You must understand where it's being invested and why, and be comfortable with these choices. That's why I want you to check out different interest rates at banks and the fees they charge. That's why I want you to be familiar with stocks, bonds, and mutual funds. You don't have to become an expert, but at least make an effort. It's your money. No one else is going to take care of it. Now I fully understand that this may seem tedious—examining banks, various accounts, loans, and investment vehicles, but this is where you get the shovel and pickax out and start to mine for your gold. Let's get started.

Choosing a Bank

A bank offers you services such as checking accounts, savings accounts, credit card services, car loans, home loans, business loans, and other financial assistance—but you should always remember that a bank is a business. Banking is not free. The bank is not there to do you any favors, so be diligent when shopping for a bank because there may be hidden fees that a casual glance over the paperwork will not catch.

First figure out what you want out of the bank. Do you want a charge card or debit card? Will it lend money for automobile purchases or housing? Or do you want a savings account, checking account, and access to ATMs?

Find out how to get free checking from this bank. Normally, banks will give you free checking if you deposit a large amount of money in an account and leave it there.

Check out the interest rates (the rate that is paid to you for the use of your money while it's in the bank) and make sure they are competitive with other banks' rates. You will also want a bank that is close to your home or place of employment. Investigate what types of fees it will charge you—is there a fee for checking, what is the overdraft penalty if you write a check without sufficient funds in your account, what is the minimum balance requirement?

Visit the banks you are interested in doing business with. The staff should be professional and courteous. Ask your friends and family where they bank and whether they are satisfied with their experience. You don't have to give your money or your kid's money to a financial institution that has poor customer service or limited hours of operation. The banking industry is hypercompetitive these days; traditional banks, community banks, and credit unions compete for your business. You are in the driver's seat, so steer yourself and your kids in the right direction.

A quick word about ATM cards: They are convenient, but in most cases you will be charged a fee if you use an ATM that does not belong to your bank. So be sure to find out where your bank's ATMs are (and if they are convenient to use when you are shopping or away from home) and use those machines instead of the ones that will tack on a fee. Also, keep track of your transactions, especially the withdrawals—those tend to sneak up on you.

Here's a good tip: If you need cash and are out shopping and don't have access to an ATM that is associated with your bank, ask for cash back when you make your purchases with your debit card. There is no charge. Don't be foolish when asking for cash back; it's coming out of your checking account, so you had better be able to cover it. This is not a credit card, so please think carefully before you exercise this strategy.

Here's a quick warning about giving your ATM card to your kids. I was waiting in line at an ATM and happened to overhear a conversation between two teenagers. They were discussing how much cash to take out of the account. One teen was saying that they only needed about $60; that should get them comfortably through their day.

The other teen wasn't so sure. He wanted to make the day special for the girls they were taking out. This young man wanted to take out $100. The other argued that he had $40 and that should cover the date, plus they made a promise to only take out $60 at the most. Well, the teen took out the $100 anyway. His reasoning was that his mother wouldn't care (it was her card!) or wouldn't miss the money. I'm guessing that the mother told her son to take out a maximum of $60. Once the kid was at the machine, though, and he felt the surge of power that the card bestowed upon him, he couldn't control himself. I'm also guessing the mother noticed the extra $40 missing. In my house that young man would never see another ATM card until it had his name on it and his money in the account. He might not be a bad kid. In fact he could be a great kid, but he broke a promise, and in the financial world promises are like contracts. You break them, you pay the price. Let's move on.

Credit Unions

You may also want to research credit unions. A credit union is a cooperative financial institution, owned and controlled by the people who use its services. The difference between a bank and a credit union is that credit unions are nonprofit institutions and are not in business to make a profit like regular banks, or so they say. I had an acquaintance who was the president of a credit union. The only thing he was interested in was bottom-line profit, as that is where he derived most of his compensation. You should make certain that the credit union you are researching is convenient for your banking purposes and offers all the services you require.

Types of Accounts

Savings accounts actually pay you for keeping your money in the account. This is where the interest rate comes in. If you are not going to use the money on a daily basis, because you are saving for a car or for school, then this would be your best bet. You don't need a lot of money to open up the account and it is a safer place to keep your money compared to hiding it in your closet or some other secret place that does not pay you interest. You can also withdraw your money at any time. I think everyone should open up a savings account. Keep a small balance in it. Deposit a few dollars a paycheck in it. I promise that it will add up.

Checking accounts allow you to deposit money and withdraw money from an insured account. Generally speaking, a checking account enables you to use personal checks in place of cash to pay debts. You can also use electronic debit cards or ATM cards to access individual accounts or make cash withdrawals. Some checking accounts pay interest, but normally that will require you to deposit a significant amount of money in the account and leave it on deposit.

Remember, you are responsible for your checking account and for keeping track of your available funds, although every month your bank will send you a bank statement and a list of written checks. You can treat these checks as receipts if you are having problems over whether or not you paid a bill. If you did, you will have the check as proof of payment. Also, you must have enough money in your checking account to cover the checks you are writing. Checks are not just paper; they represent real money, and if you write a check for an amount higher than your available balance, you will pay the consequences in the form of numerous fees and possible legal action. Bounce too many checks and the bank will close your account and report your activity to a service that may prevent you from opening another checking account with another bank.

What Is a Check?

Don't get lazy on me here; listen up. I understand that most of you know what a check is; it's not rocket science. It's important though, to understand the power that a check has in relation to your account. One lost check could mess up your account; it could also be financially devastating if the lost check is blank and ends up in the wrong hands. I've heard horror stories about people losing checks—some of them signed but without an amount filled in!

Simply put, a check is a way of communicating with your bank by informing it of what you want done with your money. When you write a check, you are letting your bank know that you want to transfer a specific amount of money from your checking account to another person, company, or organization. You can also write a check to convert some of the money that you have in your checking account into cash.

When you fill in the blank spaces on one of your checks, you are notifying the bank as to the amount of money that you want transferred and to the specific person, company, or organization that should receive it. Once you sign the check, you have given the bank authorization to do what you instructed on the check. It is simple and convenient. Another reason why checks are so common is that people can use a canceled check to prove that they paid a bill.

A **money market account** is simply another type of savings account. The difference is that these accounts usually pay higher interest rates, which is good for saving your money over a long period, but they also have higher minimum balance requirements (normally between $1,000 and $2,500). Money market accounts usually allow only a limited number of withdrawals per month and will charge you a fee if you make more withdrawals than allowed.

As with a checking account, your bank will send you a statement each month either in the mail or by e-mail if you prefer. The statement will list all of your transactions as well as any fees charged to your account and interest your money has earned. In order to make sure you didn't forget to write down any withdrawals and/or deposits, you should go through each entry in your register and compare it with the bank statement. You should also look over the bank's records to make certain that the bank did not make any mistakes regarding your account.

These days, banks are screening new customers more than ever, as there are all sorts of federal laws to guard against fraud and terrorist activities. This may delay or even eliminate the opening of one's account.

How to Open an Account

To open an account, you must provide some information to the bank. Banks do not open bank accounts without certain details about you. This is to protect them against risk and to comply with a variety of regulations. You'll need to provide simple details like your name and birthday, as well as your Social Security number. You may also need to provide a government ID or driver's license number.

If you're doing this online, which may be more convenient, you'll simply type the information into a textbox. If you open accounts in person you can hand your ID over to the banker, who will probably make photocopies of the card.

Electronic Banking

Electronic banking uses computer and electronic technology as a substitute for checks and other paper transactions. Many people think of electronic banking as 24-hour access to cash through ATMs, a way of paying their bills without having to go to the bank or receiving paychecks, which are deposited directly into checking or savings accounts.

Here are some of the basics of electronic banking:

Automated teller machines (ATMs) or 24-hour tellers are electronic terminals that let you bank almost any time. To withdraw cash, make deposits, or transfer funds between accounts, you generally insert an ATM card and enter your personal identification number (PIN). If the machine you are using is not associated with your bank, the ATM may require a surcharge, or usage fee (which might be two or three dollars). This applies to those who are not members of the specific banking institution or on transactions at remote locations. The ATM must reveal that a surcharge will be taken out of your account on the terminal screen or on a sign next to the screen. Check the rules of your institution to find out when or whether a surcharge is imposed. Also, don't forget the little story I told you about the ATM card and the teenager earlier in this chapter. Having an ATM card or credit card in someone's hands, especially if the account doesn't belong to them, makes people do crazy things.

Direct deposit lets you authorize specific regular deposits, such as paychecks and Social Security checks, to your account. This is very convenient, and you should check with your employer to see if it offers this service. If so, take advantage of it. You will not be stuck carrying around a paycheck or waiting on long lines at the bank to deposit it. You also may preauthorize direct withdrawals so that recurring bills, such as insurance premiums, mortgages, and utility bills, are paid automatically. A good trick that I recommend to increase savings is to split the direct deposit between savings and checking in a reasonable amount to cover your immediate monthly bills and forget you have the savings. By ignoring the savings it will slowly but surely increase, giving you extra money in case of an emergency.

Personal computer banking allows you to conduct many banking transactions electronically by using your personal computer. This is another benefit of electronic banking—you can do most of your transactions from your home or office. An example is that you may use your computer to view your account balance, request transfers between accounts, and pay bills electronically.

Pay-by-phone systems allow you to telephone your financial institution with directions to pay certain bills or to transfer funds between accounts. You must first have an agreement with the institution to make such transfers.

Types of Loans

Personal loan: A personal loan is taken to meet your specific personal needs. Personal loans can be tricky; interest rates are usually very high and there are also other costs that will drive up the total amount of money you pay back compared to the sum you actually borrow. You could accumulate costs for processing of the loan, underwriting, and credit report fees, as well as late fees if you do not make timely payments. The bank will also have strict requirements before it lends you this money—meaning that you will need good credit, verification of income, and/or proof of other assets. It helps to have a business relationship with the bank in the form of a checking or savings account.

Auto loan: The dealer you are working with usually can procure you an auto loan—depending on your credit history, which you will be working on improving. If you decide to go directly with a bank and not with what the dealership proposes, carefully compare the loan programs that are offered and read the fine print. If a loan sounds too good to be true, then it probably is. Understand one thing, though: The purchase price the salesperson gives you will not be the total price you pay in the end. The annual percentage rate (APR) and other fees will balloon the price over the period that you have decided to take the loan. For instance, taking a four- or five-year loan will add thousands to the original price. The APR is sometimes as important as the type of car that you will be buying. As a matter of fact, if you like two cars just about the same, the car that has the lower APR should be your choice.

Home loan: Obviously a home loan is used to buy a home, but there are many factors involved. You will have to show a good credit score, which provides evidence of your ability to pay back money you owe. I understand that this is a work in progress but as I stated before, you can't learn enough about money matters. The lender will analyze your ability to repay the mortgage based on the monthly payment, which will include property taxes and insurance on the property, plus existing monthly bills. The bank will also review your liquid finances. You will have to have proof of an income that can cover the loan and your other financial obligations. There are many home loans, so you should be very careful and do your research to find the loan that will not only benefit you now but also in the future.

Home equity loans: A home equity loan allows a homeowner to borrow against the equity built up in the house. The homeowner is taking a loan out against the value of his or her home. A good method of determining the amount of home equity available for a loan would be to take the difference between the home's market value and the amount still owed on the mortgage. The loan proceeds may be used for any number of reasons, but they are usually used for home improvement purposes or for building home additions, but some use this money to consolidate their debt. Home equity loans normally command a higher interest rate as a result of the increase risk associated with them in terms of collateral priority.

Signature loan: A signature loan is an unsecured personal loan given at a fixed rate. Since there is no security that the bank can seize, the bank strictly requires that borrowers have good credit, a good income, and financial stability before granting this type of loan. These loans are used when you need cash for bill consolidation, auto repairs, vacations, emergency cash, taxes, or other personal financial needs. As with most personal loans it does help if you have a business relationship with the bank—as in a checking or savings account or if you have paid back a previous loan with the bank.

Investing Your Money

Certificate of deposit accounts (CD) are a place to put your savings for a fixed period—until the CD matures, which can range from only a few weeks to several years. The longer the time period for maturity, the greater the amount of interest you will receive on your money. Keep in mind that you cannot touch this money as you could in a savings account or other accounts, so you should be positive that you can live without the money you invest in a CD. Also, there are no check-writing privileges on the money; once it is invested it is there for the duration. Note, if you withdraw the funds prior to the maturity date you may be assessed an early withdrawal penalty. This penalty may negate your investment return.

Savings bonds are a way for the government to borrow money. Just like individuals and large corporations, the government needs to borrow money occasionally. In essence you are lending money and the government is agreeing to pay the money back at a fixed rate of interest over a fixed period. The purchase price is one half of the face value of the bond. For example, a $100 bond costs $50. Bonds are great for protecting your principal, saving for a child's education, giving as a gift, or generating tax-deferred income for retirement.

Traditional individual retirement accounts (IRA) are unique in that they allow you to make tax-deductible contributions. Your money, through the account, can be invested in stocks, bonds, mutual funds, and other financial vehicles, and the earnings grow tax-free. There is a catch: You must wait until you turn 59 1/2; you will then be allowed to start withdrawing money from the account to help with your retirement. If you withdraw money before you turn 59 1/2, you will be penalized a rate of 10 percent plus you will be responsible for paying tax on the amount withdrawn. Between the income tax at current rates and the penalty, you may end up paying as much as 45 percent, which means you could get as little as 55 cents on every dollar withdrawn. Even though there may be exceptions to this rule, I suggest that you never touch the money you put away for retirement—it's simply not a smart move.

With **Roth individual retirement accounts** you will not receive an income-tax deduction in the year when you make the contribution. If you happen to need some money from your account, you can withdraw the principal at any time (although you will pay penalties if you withdraw any of the earnings your money has made). The appealing thing about the Roth IRA is that when you reach retirement age, you will be able to withdraw all of the money tax-free. Thus your money grows for free. Unfortunately, there are requirements to be met in order to qualify for a Roth IRA. You can easily educate yourself on these requirements by searching on the Web at IRS.gov.

Regardless of which IRA you choose, it can be opened through a bank or brokerage house. Make sure that you research your options before you open an account. You may need a broker if you are interested in holding stocks or bonds in your IRA. Another good thing is that an IRA is easy to open and it's even easier to make contributions.

Mutual Funds

When you invest in a mutual fund, you and other investors will be pooling your money with the help of a fund manager. The fund manager is responsible for investing the collective money into specific securities (usually stocks or bonds). When you invest in a mutual fund, you are buying shares of the mutual fund, and you become a shareholder of the fund. You will be paying a fee for the work that your fund manager does—namely buying the stocks and bonds that best meet the objectives of the fund.

Here is something to consider. It has been documented that because of the fees that you pay when investing in mutual funds—the sales force of the company you are working with, its marketing, trading costs, and so forth—many mutual funds do not perform as well as the average return of the stock market.

With mutual funds you're taxed on dividends earned as well as gains from securities the fund bought and sold, and later, when you sell your shares of a fund, you pay taxes on the difference between your purchase price and the current price of fund shares. You should keep a record of all purchases. It would be wise if you did some serious research on mutual funds before you jump in and start investing your money. As such, you should always try to seek out a mutual fund with lower fees and decent performances. Investing in the stock market is risky; however, great rewards can be gained over time. Investing is not a race. It is a slow crawl, one that may take years to meet your goals.

You know what it's like to lose your money so now, when you are starting over, be wise, educated, diligent, and informed. You be the boss. As I said before, you are usually on your own when making choices regarding your money. There will be other professionals who say they are there to guide and assist you, and in all fairness, they could be, but in the end if something goes wrong it will be your money lost, not theirs. Be wary and above all read everything, especially the fine print. And if you don't understand something, ask questions. I don't care who you are working with, a bank associate or someone selling mutual funds; if they can't answer your questions in a clear, concise manner, they are not the person you should be doing business with.

Your money deserves the required attention it takes (and it takes a lot) in order to capitalize on the vast possibilities that could evolve from your arrangements and transactions. If you read this section carefully you will have noticed that there are a variety of fees that you could be charged if you aren't careful.

Chapter SEVEN

Continuing on Your Financial Freedom Quest

You've heard the saying "You learn something new every day." Well, you can apply that to your financial education. The banks, credit card companies, retailers, and advertisers are constantly thinking about how they can make more money. That money comes from people like you and me—whether we spend it wisely or foolishly, invest it, or use it to sustain a healthy retirement. We must keep up with the financial conglomerates that are setting the rules, or making new rules up, in order to be smart with our money and become empowered.

There's simply no other way to put it: You must keep your eye on the prize or risk losing everything again. Let me tell you a story of a husband and wife who were clients of mine. After they lost nearly everything, they started to do what was necessary to correct their situation. They made lists before they went food shopping and stuck to the lists; they used coupons and bought store-brand items; they stopped going out for dinner or lunch—they did it all. They even reduced the number of cars they owned to one used vehicle. The husband found someone he could car pool with for a small amount of gas money each week.

Once they got themselves back on their feet, they started to become lazy. She found another job that paid more and instead of saving that extra money, as if it never existed, which is a smart way to look at it, they wiped that gain out completely by buying a new car. Now they were in the same predicament they were in when she had her old job—making just enough money to pay the bills and not enough to save. They didn't learn their lesson, and instead of staying diligent they became too comfortable.

That comfort didn't last long. The older car broke down and they needed money to fix it. They had just enough, but that wiped out their savings. If they would have saved that extra earned money instead of buying a new car their problem would have been easily solved. Soon other unexpected bills began to pop up and they didn't have the money to pay them. In just over a year they lost the new car to the repo man and their credit was completely shot. This couple had a second chance but they let it slip away, all because they couldn't control their spending again.

This could have been a different scenario. The wife could have found a new job and bought a new car and then her husband might have fallen ill. Then the issues would have been hospital bills and his inability to work and earn money. You see it can happen at any time and in any shape or form. You never know when a disaster is going to occur, but you can prepare for that disaster to the best of your ability. Don't just wait and react; be pro-active now that you have decided to become more financially savvy.

Okay, enough with the horror stories. Let's discuss some ways you can save money and help the environment. It's really a win-win situation.

Find Your Green

It seems strange to me that creating a healthier, more vibrant environment isn't always a priority. It's common sense—once the air, earth, and water go foul, all creatures die, including us. Of course, you have special-interest groups that care more about making money than taking care of the earth and its inhabitants, even their own children, it seems . . . but that's for another book. For right now let's try to do our part and save some money along the way. I have come up with a list of things that you can do to prevent unnecessary pollutants from contaminating our earth, air, and water while also banking some cash.

Although I may not come across as an avid outdoorsman, the environment is worth preserving as we only have one shot at this. There is no do-over with Mother Nature. By following some of these tips you will save money either immediately or in the long run, and that suits our purposes. Also, I completely understand that not all of these things will be relevant to everyone (my family only uses a portion of these methods), but even if you can adopt a dozen or so ideas, you'll become more efficient in spending and saving your hard-earned money.

Okay, let's get started:

- Adjust your thermostat to a lower temperature in the winter and a higher temperature in the summer. Don't groan; you can wear a sweater in the winter or open the windows at times during the spring and summer.

- Weather-strip and caulk your home. Be certain that there are no areas by the windows and doors that allow the outdoor temperature to interfere with your indoor comfort.
- Open your curtains or blinds/shades in the winter to let in the warmth of the sun.
- Close the doors in each room so the heat or air conditioning won't escape.
- Close curtains/blinds/shades in the summer to keep the heat out.
- Keep clean air filters in your air conditioning system and in the vents, if necessary. Clean filters allow more air to flow into the home and also maintain cleaner air.
- Use rechargeable batteries. You can find them where you buy regular batteries. They cost more but will save you money in the long run.
- Use power strips for your TV, radio, computer, and so forth and keep them turned off when not in use.
- Open the door to your dishwasher and let the air dry the dishes instead of running the machine's heater.
- Keep the refrigerator door shut. You don't need to open it a half dozen times to figure out what you want.
- Fix any water leaks in the bathroom or kitchen—wherever you have a faucet or toilet. You can't imagine how much water is wasted when there is a leak.
- Purchase low-flow shower heads. These may cost a bit more in the beginning but the savings will be worth it down the road.

- Turn the water off while you are brushing your teeth, shaving, or washing your face.
- Reduce your garbage. Many of the things that are thrown out can either be recycled or put into a compost bin to produce mulch/fertilizer. Items such as eggshells, fruit peels, and coffee grounds are ideal.
- Buy reusable washcloths or towels to use for cleanup in the kitchen rather than paper towels. This will save lots of money and go a long way in helping the environment.
- Use cloth bags instead of plastic bags when you go to the food store. Plastic bags are incredibly destructive to wildlife—fish, turtles, and other marine life choke on these bags. Some of these plastics end up in our waterways. Plastic bags also take hundreds of years to biodegrade.
- Replace your plastic water bottles with reusable bottles such as canteen-type containers. Plastic water bottles plague the environment and you are paying a high price for water you can get at your sink!
- If you don't feel comfortable drinking tap water, purchase a small water filtration system. In the long run, it will save you money.
- Replace burned-out bulbs with energy-efficient bulbs. They do cost a bit more but they last much longer and use less energy. That means saving money. The law changed anyway; incandescent bulbs are being phased out over the next few years.
- When possible, buy in bulk to not only save money but also to diminish the use of packaging material used.

- Use cleaners that are environmentally friendly. Even the top brands are selling "green" cleaners at reasonable prices. They also won't spread harmful chemicals around your home.
- Burn candles in your home instead of using air fresheners. Candles evoke a pleasant atmosphere and they don't have all the harmful chemicals that the sprays contain. Be careful not to burn your home down.
- You can search the Internet for homemade cleaners that use vinegar, baking soda, water, and lemon juice as ingredients. They work just as well, and the nasty chemicals in regular cleaners will be reduced.
- Purchase reusable coffee filters instead of buying filters that you use once and throw away—what a waste of money and it just adds to your garbage.
- Use cloth napkins instead of buying paper napkins. They are more expensive at first but just think how much money you will save over a year!
- Buy reusable containers for sandwiches and snacks for the kids' lunches or for your own lunch. You can find all kinds of products at your grocery store. This will save you money (you won't have to keep purchasing plastic bags).
- Get a reusable coffee cup or mug. Many places that sell coffee offer these mugs, and you can sometimes get a discount on the coffee if you use the mug. Better yet, make your own coffee with reusable coffee filters, and you will save even more money and aid

the environment by reducing the amount of garbage thrown away.

- Purchase your fruits and vegetable at a farmers market. You won't believe how much money you will save and you will also be giving back to your local producers. You will be cutting back on shipping, which reduces the amount of gas used and carbon monoxide produced.
- If a market is not close, purchase fresh produce instead of canned or plastic-packaged. You will be putting less garbage back into the environment, and the fresh produce tastes better.
- Purchase bar soap rather than liquid soap that comes in plastic bottles—again with the plastic! Plastic ends up polluting unless you recycle it diligently, and you can also probably find some decent prices on bar soap. Also, I don't know this for sure, but I bet bar soaps last longer than soft soaps. Soaps in plastic bottles just invite you to pour it out and lather up.
- Don't wash your bath towels after one use. You can get a few uses out of them and still be hygienic. You'll end up wasting too much water and paying for it at the end of the month. Additionally, the more you wash towels and sheets, the quicker the fabric deteriorates.
- Instead of spraying insecticides, buy a birdhouse or two for your yard. Birds love to eat insects and they add charm to your landscape. If you are handy, build your own birdhouse. That may be a fun challenge for the kids, too.

- Don't use chemicals to kill weeds. Get out in the yard and enjoy the nice weather. Sure, weeding is not the most exciting way to spend a morning or afternoon, but it's better for you than sitting on the couch watching television snacking on junk food or spraying poisonous chemicals around your yard. Those chemicals end up getting washed down the street drains and eventually end up in ponds, streams, or rivers. Weeding is also a lot less expensive than chemicals.

- Use a push mower on your lawn. There are some neat push mowers on the market and they won't cost you as much as an electric- or gas-powered mower. Plus you'll be getting some exercise.

- Recycle the paper you use at work and at home. You can purchase recycled paper for office or home use.

- When you're done using your computer, turn it off. Don't leave it in sleep mode. Also, turn off your monitor. Leaving your computer on all the time may cost you almost $100 annually.

- Turn off the lights in rooms that you are not using. Turn off ceiling fans when you leave your home. They don't need to run constantly.

- I know some people who leave their TV on all day for their pets. That's not a good idea. It's a huge waste of energy and money. I'm sure your pet can do without the soap operas! Too much stress brought on from all the drama, plus you might burn out your TV sooner.

- Recycle ink cartridges for your printer. Some stores have recycling programs that offer lower prices for cartridges, and they also take your old cartridges.

- Recycle all the cans, bottles, and paper that you use in the house. If your town doesn't have a recycling program, find a town nearby that does. You may be able to take your recyclables there and make a few extra bucks.
- Use public transportation. This will save wear and tear on your vehicle, and it also saves gas.
- Get a bicycle. You could probably find a used one cheap in the local paper. You can use the bike for errands and keep your heart and body in good condition.
- Maintain your vehicle. Make certain the air pressure in your tires is correct; change the oil regularly and check the air filter. These small tasks can help save gas, which in turn leaves you with extra money.
- Make a list of your daily or weekly errands and do them in an efficient manner. Don't make multiple trips to the store; you'll only end up wasting gas and time and you'll probably spend more money.
- Offer to carpool with coworkers. Send an e-mail to those who live within a reasonable distance of your home and see what type of response you receive.
- Save gas by slowing down. Why are we all in such a hurry?
- When you are in the market for a new vehicle, look for one that gets great gas mileage—don't get sucked into the "cool" car or one that you can't afford. Remember what we discussed in the earlier chapters about cars. Be careful when purchasing an electric car. You want to make sure that the premium you're paying will be outweighed by the gas savings down the road.

- Don't have your newspaper delivered and don't bother buying one at the store. You can get the news via your Internet, sometimes at no charge. That makes it cheaper and it saves on paper. Why cut down another tree if we don't have to?

Okay, so that's about it. You may not be able to use all of these ideas, but there are at least a dozen that you can adopt to save money and be more environmentally friendly. As a side note, I recently dusted off my old bicycle. I'm not a young man anymore but I decided to go for a ride to my friend's house. I would usually drive the five miles to his home when we get together. Let me tell you, it was liberating! I loved it and I still love it. A couple of my buddies laughed at first, but now they are using peddle power when they visit me or run a light errand.

It's a great way to get outside, exercise, and get out of the car. We spend so much time in our cars that it seems the whole world is locked outside. With my bike I'm out in the world; I can feel the sun and the breeze. It really is wonderful. If you don't bike already, I highly recommend it.

It's Time to Step Out on Your Own

Now that we learned a few methods for keeping your path cleaner, it's time to start thinking about taking back your financial power. I sincerely hope that you have learned something from this book. If there is one thing that you can take away, although I think you can take more than a single notion away, it's that you are mostly on your own. Of course, you have your family and friends, and you have me as a resource, but ultimately it's you who has to do the work and make the changes. I don't want this to sound cruel, but it's the harsh reality: No one else will take care of your money except you. Other people may *take* your money, but they won't necessarily do what's in your best interest.

Remember, it's your money. You can watch it disappear and continue to have that awful feeling of being broke, or you can be smart and start saving it and making it work for you. I am obviously very acquainted with credit counseling services and people who have lost their life savings. It's brutal and that's why I chose to share my experiences with all of you. In the end there is only you—and I want you to make the right choices now that you are starting all over again. Make a pact with yourself, be determined, and realize that you are on the precipice of a life-changing moment. This is your chance to erase the past and welcome a prosperous future.

You probably feel like you've been locked in a room that you could not get out of, you could not find the exit. You've been trapped by debt. You've been overwhelmed by the deluge of bills, phone calls from debt collectors, the worries that cascade through your mind and hamper your ability to function properly. The humiliation and embarrassment, the feelings of "why me" and "how could this happen," have reverberated in your skull for too long. I'm telling you now that the door is here, right in front of you, and I want you to open the door and get out of that room. I want you to free yourself of your burdens and start fresh. Learn from what happened in the past but don't dwell on it, because it's over. Because of your past, you are a new person, a stronger, better-informed person, and a more resilient and educated person.

Now is the time to educate yourself, and by reading this book you have taken that first step. What a wonderful thing to be given another chance. You are free to make the decisions necessary to reinvent yourself as a savvy financial individual. No one can take that away from you now. You have paid the price, and now I want you to be a motivated person. Keep progressing, even when doubt starts to whisper in your ear, until you are solvent again, and once that happens continue on because it will never end. As long as there is money, credit cards, banks, bills, and products to buy, you will be treading on your personal path to financial independence. This is now a tangible part of your life, so embrace it—go for it!

I wish you the best of luck. I have seen people rise from the worst possible financial catastrophes and become successful again. I hope and I trust that you too will be one of those people shortly. If you need support, read this book over and over and you will find it. I will be here in these pages rooting for you, challenging you, and pushing you forward.

Now that you've opened the door, take a deep breath, and say goodbye to the past. Begin to live a new life—a life of meaning, a life with less stress than the one you left behind, a life where you're in control.

Glossary

In this glossary, you will find definitions for commonly used terms related to credit and debt. Knowing what these terms mean will help you make informed decisions about your finances.

Acceleration Clause. A provision in a loan agreement that allows a creditor to demand payment in full if you do not meet the terms of the agreement.

Accrued Interest. Interest that accumulates on a debt that you owe.

Annual Percentage Rate (APR). The cost of credit, expressed as a yearly rate. The federal Truth in Lending Act requires that all offers for credit indicate the credit's APR so that consumers can understand the cost of the credit they are applying for and so they can compare credit offers.

Balloon Payment. A final payment on a loan that is substantially larger than previous payments.

Bankruptcy. A legal procedure governed by federal law that helps consumers who have too much debt. If you file for Chapter 13, you will have three to five years to pay off your debts, and the balance of what you owe on certain debts will be wiped out at the end of that time. Some debts will remain. If you file for Chapter 11, you will have to give up certain assets so that they can be sold and the proceeds will be applied to your debts.

Cash Advance. Cash obtained from a credit card.

Cash Value. The savings portion of a whole life, universal, or variable life insurance policy. You can borrow against that value.

Closed-End Credit. A loan that you must repay by making fixed payments over a specified period.

Collection Agency. A business that collects past-due debts for other businesses and individuals. Most collection agencies get paid for their services by taking a percentage of what they collect for their clients.

Collateral. Assets pledged as security for a secured debt. If you do not pay a debt that you have collateralized, the creditor can take the collateral.

Cosigner. Someone who signs a credit agreement. If the main borrower does not repay the debt according to the terms of the agreement, the creditor can look to that other person for payment. The main borrower and the cosigner are equally responsible for the debt.

Credit Agreement. A contract between a borrower and a creditor that details the amount borrowed, the applicable interest rate, and all other terms of the credit.

Credit Bureau. A business that gathers information regarding consumers' use of credit and provides that information to businesses and organizations legally authorized to review it. Also called a credit reporting agency.

Credit History. A record of how you have managed your credit that is maintained by a credit bureau. Creditors, insurers, employers, and landlords use consumer credit record information as well as credit scores based on that information to make decisions about consumers. Also called a credit record, credit report, or credit file.

Credit Insurance. Insurance that repays a loan in the event of your death or disability.

Credit Practices Rule. This rule protects you when you apply for credit with a retail business, auto dealer, credit union, or finance company by requiring the lender to include specific disclosures in its consumer credit contracts. The disclosures relate to your rights should you fail to repay the credit according to the contract's terms. It also requires that you be provided with certain written information if you agree to cosign someone else's credit and gives you specific rights when it comes to late fees.

Credit Repair. The process of removing inaccurate or outdated information from your credit record. Some credit repair firms use illegal methods to remove negative but accurate information from consumers' credit files.

Credit Repair Organizations Act. A federal law that regulates the activities of credit repair organizations and that gives consumers specific rights when they work with such an organization.

Credit Score. A number that is derived from the information in your credit history and that is an indicator of how well you are likely to manage credit in the future.

Creditor. A person or business to whom you owe money.

Debit Card. A card that allows you to pay for purchases out of your bank account or money market account without writing a check. The money for the purchase may come directly out of your account at the time of purchase or your account may be debited for the cost of the transaction a couple days later if you use the card like a charge card.

Debt Consolidation. The process of taking out a larger loan to pay off one or more smaller loans.

Default. What you do when you do not live up to the terms of a credit agreement.

Default Judgment. A court judgment issued by a judge when you are sued and don't respond to the lawsuit.

Deficiency. The difference between what you owe on a secured debt and what the asset that secures it sells for.

Discharge. What happens when the court erases certain debts at the end of your bankruptcy so that you will not have to pay them.

Down Payment. The initial amount of money you may have to pay when you make a credit purchase. For example, you make a down payment on a home. The down payment reduces the amount that you must finance and helps protects the lender should you default on your credit agreement.

Electronic Funds Transfer Act. A federal law that provides you with limited protections when unauthorized purchases and withdrawals are made using your ATM or debit card or when errors related to purchases and withdrawals you made with your ATM or debit card appear on your bank statement.

Equal Credit Opportunity Act. A federal act that prohibits creditors from discriminating against you during the credit application process on the basis of your race, religion, national origin, sex, age, or marital status, or because you receive public assistance. It also requires creditors to respond to your credit application within 30 days of receiving it. If you are denied credit or granted less credit than you applied for, the law requires that the creditor give you a specific reason why.

Equity. The difference between what your home is worth and the balance due on your mortgage and on any other financial obligations that your home may secure.

Exempt Assets. The assets you are allowed to keep if a creditor gets a legal judgment against you because you have not paid a debt or if you file for bankruptcy. Every state has a law that spells out the types of assets consumers can claim as exempt. There are federal exemptions too.

Fair Credit Billing Act. A federal act that establishes procedures for correcting billing errors when you purchase a product or service using a credit card or retail store charge card. The law also protects you when someone you did not authorize uses your credit card or retail store charge. The law also protects you when you purchase merchandise with a credit card or retail store charge card and the merchandise turns out to be defective, damaged, shoddily made, or not delivered, or if you pay for a service with your credit card or retail store charge and the service is not delivered or not provided according to the terms of your contract.

Fair Credit and Charge Card Disclosure Act.   Part of the federal Truth in Lending Act, this law requires creditors to provide you with specific information when you apply for credit or when they send you an offer for credit so that you know how much the credit will cost you to use and so you can compare credit offers.

Fair Credit Reporting Act.   A federal act that gives consumers specific rights when it comes to the information in their credit histories. It also establishes specific responsibilities for credit bureaus, suppliers of information to credit bureaus, and users of that information.

Fair Debt Collection Practices Act.   A federal law that regulates the activities of debt collectors and establishes your rights when you are contacted by a debt collector.

Finance Charge.   The cost of consumer credit expressed as a percentage rate.

Forbearance.   When a creditor agrees not to collect on a debt.

Foreclosure.   The process whereby a mortgage lender or another creditor with a lien on your home or on some other piece of real estate that you own takes that asset because you did not live up to the terms of your agreement with the creditor.

Grace Period.   The period during which you can pay your account balance in full without incurring a finance charge.

Home Equity Line of Credit. A type of credit that allows you to tap the equity in your home as needed up to a certain dollar amount. Your home serves as collateral.

Home Equity Loan Consumer Protection Act. A law that requires a creditor to provide you with certain information when you apply for a home equity line of credit so that you can understand the true cost of the credit and can compare it to similar offers.

Identity Theft and Assumption Deterrence Act. This law makes stealing your identity a criminal act and establishes your rights when you are the victim of identity fraud.

Installment Loan. A loan that you repay over time by making payments of principle and interest at specific intervals.

Judgment. The court's decision at the end of a lawsuit.

Judgment Proof. When you have no assets that a creditor can take to satisfy a judgment against you.

Lien. A creditor's claim against property you own. When a creditor has a lien on one of your assets, if you do not pay the debt that is associated with that lien, the creditor has a legal right to take the property. Your mortgage lender has a lien against your home and your car lender has a lien on your car.

Mortgage Loan. A loan to purchase real estate. The loan is secured by the real estate.

Open-end Credit Agreement. A credit agreement with no specific date by which you must pay the account balance in full although you must make monthly minimum payments on the balance. Credit cards are a common example of open-ended credit, as are retail store charge cards and gasoline cards.

Periodic Rate.   An interest rate that changes periodically. The terms of the change are spelled out in your credit agreement.

Personal Property.   An asset that can be moved, as opposed to real estate, which is fixed. Your personal property may include vehicles, furniture, jewelry, fine art, and so on.

Prepayment Penalty.   A penalty that may apply if you pay off a loan early. The penalty compensates the lender for the fact that it will not earn as much interest income on the loan as if you had continued paying on it until the loan term was up.

Principal.   The amount of money you borrow. Principal does not include interest.

Punitive Damages.   Money that a court may order a business to pay you as punishment for harming you in some way and to encourage the business not to repeat its illegal behavior.

Refinance.   To pay off an existing loan and get a new loan in order to lower your interest rate, get more or less time to pay off the loan, and so forth. You may also refinance as a way to raise cash.

Repossession.   When a secured creditor takes back your collateral—your car, for example—because you did not live up to your agreement with the creditor.

Secured Credit Card. A credit card that is secured by money in your savings account or by a CD. You can borrow only up to a percentage of the money in the account or the value of your CD. If you do not pay on your credit card according to the terms of your credit agreement, the creditor can take the funds in your savings account or your CD.

Secured Creditor. A creditor that has a lien on one of your assets. If you do not pay the creditor according to the terms of your agreement, the creditor is entitled to take the asset, also referred to as collateral.

Secured Debt. A debt that you collateralized with an asset that you own. If you do not meet the terms of your credit agreement, the lender can take that asset in payment. Common examples of secured debts include car loans and mortgages.

Security Agreement. An agreement associated with a secured loan. The agreement specifies the collateral that secures the loan and under what circumstances the creditor can take the collateral, among other things.

Term. The length of time that a loan agreement will be in effect—from the date that the agreement is signed to the date that the loan will be paid in full.

Truth in Lending Act. A federal law that requires specific disclosures about the terms of credit so that consumers can make informed decisions regarding whether a particular credit offer is a good deal for them. It also gives you a variety of other rights when you apply for or use credit.

Unsecured Debt. A debt for which no assets are pledged to guarantee payment. The most common type of unsecured debt is credit card debt.

Usury Laws. State laws that regulate the interest rates that creditors can charge consumers.

Wage Garnishment. What may happen if you do not pay a debt that you owe. The creditor you owe the money to will get a judgment against you and then get the court's permission to take a percentage of your wages in order to get its money. Your employer will be legally required to deduct the garnishment amount from your paychecks. Not all states permit wage garnishment.

About the Author

Howard S. Dvorkin CPA is a serial entrepreneur, a two-time author, and a personal finance expert. With the successful international expansion of his organizations, he focused his professional endeavors in the consumer finance, technology, media and real estate industries. As the Founder of Consolidated Credit Howard is one of the most highly regarded debt and credit expert in the United States and has played an instrumental role in drafting both State and Federal Legislation. Howard's success in the personal finance industry landed him column in Fox Business News as well as has allowed him to be interviewed by countless media outlets over the years including the Wall Street Journal, the New York Times, Fortune, Entrepreneur, The American Banker, Investor's Business Daily, and virtually every national and local newspaper in the country. He has also appeared as a finance expert on national and local television and radio programs, including the CBS Nightly News, ABC World News Tonight, The Early Show, Fox News, and CNN.

In his latest book, *Power Up: Taking Charge of Your Financial Destiny*, he takes on the challenge of helping people who are financially stuck. In this book Howard revolutionizes the way people think about shopping, advertising, "keeping up with the Joneses," values, credit cards, spending money, and more. If you have suffered the tragedy of losing everything because of a job loss, medical bills, or a combination of factors, you are not alone. Howard understands that and competently steers you in the direction of financial rebirth. He guides you through this emotional time with expertise, wisdom, and compassion because he has encountered it with thousands of others and assisted them by imparting the knowledge that over two decades of experience in the industry brings.

With Howard's guidance, Consolidated Credit won the 2012 Excellence in Financial Literacy Education (EIFLE) Nonprofit Organization of the Year Award. He is a consultant to the Board of Directors for the Association of Credit Counseling Professionals (ACCPros) and is the past president of the Association of Independent Consumer Credit Counseling Agencies (AICCCA).

Howard has been honored by many organizations and has been named a 2014 Laureate in the Junior Achievement Business Hall of Fame, which honors community leaders who have achieved business excellence, vision and innovation while inspiring courageous leadership and community responsibility. He was as named Heavy Hitter of the Year by The South Florida Business Journal and is a two-time nominee for the Ernst and Young Entrepreneur of the Year Award. He continually dedicates his time to the National Leadership Council at American University and the Kogod School of Business inducted him into the prestigious 1923 Society at American University. He has been the recipient of the South Florida Diamond Award as well as the Ben Gurion Award.

About the Author

Howard graduated from the University of Miami with a Master's Degree in Business Administration and received his Bachelor of Science Degree in Accounting from American University. He is currently listed in the Marquis Who's Who in the Finance Industry and is part of the premier group of CPAs that are recognized with the Chartered Global Management Accountant (CGMA) designation.

Index